PRAISE FOR KI PORTER

Ki Porter has given the world a stellar debut.

— VELLUM REVIEWS

A scalpel in a drawer full of knives.

— THAT GUY WHO'S ALWAYS AT STARBUCKS

With a blend of wit and charm, Ki Porter is a modern-day Jane Austen.

— BEN REEDING

YOU CAN DO IT

ACCESS YOUR FAITH

KI PORTER

PREFACE

As I sit down to write this book, I am filled with a sense of awe and gratitude for the amazing grace of God that has sustained me through some of the most difficult moments of my life. My name is Ki Porter, and I am a witness to the power of faith and the resilience of a Spiritual Experience.

My journey has been marked by moments of extreme pain and loss, but also by moments of triumph and victory. I have seen firsthand the darkest aspects of humanity, from the senseless violence of domestic abuse to the heartbreak of losing a bestfriend, spouse, and child. Yet, I have also seen the light of hope and the power of love, which have helped me to rise above the challenges and keep moving forward.

One of the most traumatic experiences of my life was witnessing the murder of my best friend at the hands of her boyfriend, who then dug her grave in his grandmother's backyard. This event left me feeling numb and helpless, wondering how such evil could exist in the world. But it was also a turning point in my life, as it led me to seek out a deeper connection with God and to discover the strength within myself to overcome adversity.

Unfortunately, the challenges that one can face in life can be overwhelming and seemingly never-ending. I'm a victim of a hit that was intended to kill my husband. To make matters worse, I was falsely accused of crimes and had to fight to clear my name in court, which came with exorbitant legal fees. This ordeal even led to being featured on America's Most Wanted. For one person, the difficulties did not end after becoming a young widow. The loss of a child followed and truly challenged my faith.

Despite these traumatic experiences, I refused to let them break me. My faith has been tested, but I persevered through the pain and loss that I still grieve to this day. Through it all, I have learned that we are capable of more than we ever thought possible. We can endure the unthinkable and come out stronger on the other side. This book is my testament to that truth, and my hope is that it will inspire and encourage others who may be going through difficult times of their own.

So to anyone reading this, know that you can do it. You can overcome the challenges in your life, no matter how daunting they may seem. You have within you the strength, the courage, and the faith to keep moving forward, even when the path ahead is dark. I pray that my story will help you to find that inner light and to never give up hope.

FOREWORD

Title: You Can Do It: How to Access Your Faith

Kiki Porter has written a book to encourage your heart and help you walk in victory! Kiki maps out a life of greater happiness, growing in faith and using our faith more fully. This book draws you closer to discovering your deepest purpose—and living it.

I have known Kiki for years, as a close friend and a leader in our church, and I can tell you: she doesn't just talk the talk, she sings it! Her powerful ministry of praise and worship helps us lift up our hearts to the Lord and put our hands in his, rejoice in his goodness and say yes from our hearts to his will and his way. We experience this whenever Kiki sings and testifies.

But she doesn't just talk it and sing it, she *lives* it. I have seen firsthand how Kiki has overcome obstacles and flourished—even in difficult times—by living out the principles she distills in this book. God has brought breakthrough after breakthrough in Kiki's life... and when she declares and describes his goodness, you can't help shedding some tears and trusting him more.

Kiki is a living testimony to God's keeping care and miraculous intervention. Her faith shines, and in its light all of us who know her see new possibilities for our lives. She reminds us that God is able, and she models the kind of faith we can use to position ourselves for the victory he has in store. Wherever you are in your journey, whatever your religious background or experience, this book is for you! You'll gain insight and practical steps you can follow for twenty-one days of transformation.

Read this book... absorb it... follow Kiki's lead, and move ahead in faith, purpose, and victory!

Rev. Dr. Michael Woodcock
First Baptist Church of North Hollywood

INTRODUCTION

Faith is a powerful force that can transform your life. It can help overcome obstacles, achieve your goals, and find peace in difficult times. But accessing your faith can be challenging, especially if you are facing doubts or struggles. This book is designed to help you tap into your inner strength and access your faith, so you can live a fulfilling and joyful life. Faith is a powerful force that has shaped human history and transformed countless lives.

It is a belief in something greater than us, a trust in the unseen, and a conviction that there is a purpose to our existence. From the dawn of civilization, faith has been a driving force behind the creation of cultures, the formation of societies, and the quest for knowledge and meaning. The power of faith lies not only in its ability to inspire and motivate individuals, but also in its capacity to bring people together in common purpose. Faith has the power to create communities of like-minded individuals who share common values and beliefs, and who are committed to a shared vision of the world.

Faith is a deeply personal and an individual belief

system that can provide a wide range of benefits to those who embrace it. For many people, faith is a source of comfort, guidance, and inspiration that helps them navigate life's challenges with a sense of purpose and direction. This book, will explore some of the key benefits of having faith and how it can positively impact and change our lives.

- Provides a sense of purpose and meaning.

One of the primary benefits of having faith is that it can provide a sense of purpose and meaning to our lives. When we believe in something greater than ourselves, it can help us to see our place in the world and understand our role in the grand scheme of things. This can provide us with a sense of direction and help us to live a more meaningful life.

- Brings comfort in difficult times.

Life can be unpredictable and challenging, and there are times when we all face difficult situations that can leave us feeling lost and alone. Having faith can provide a sense of comfort and solace during these times, reminding us that we are not alone and that there is always hope.

- Encourages forgiveness and compassion.

Many faiths promote forgiveness and compassion as core values, and embracing these principles can have a positive impact on our relationships with others. When we can forgive those who have wronged us and show compassion to those who are suffering, it can lead to greater understanding and empathy, strengthening our connections to those around us.

- Promotes inner peace and well-being.

Faith can also have a positive impact on our mental and emotional well-being, promoting feelings of inner peace and contentment. When we have faith, we are often better able to manage stress and anxiety, and we may be more resilient in the face of challenges.

- Provides a sense of community.

Many faiths also provide a sense of community, offering opportunities for fellowship and connection with others who share our beliefs. This sense of community can be a powerful source of support and encouragement, especially during difficult times.

- Offers guidance and wisdom.

Faith can also provide us with guidance and wisdom as we navigate the complexities of life. Many faiths offer a set of principles or teachings that can help us make decisions, and they may also provide us with role models or stories that inspire us to be our best selves.

There are many benefits to having faith, ranging from a sense of purpose, and meaning to inner peace and well-being. Whether we turn to religion, spirituality, or a personal belief system, having faith can help us to navigate life's challenges with greater ease and resilience, and it can also provide us with a sense of connection to something greater than ourselves.

The phrase "faith without works is dead" is a common phrase used in the Christian faith, particularly among those who believe in the importance of living out their faith through good works. The phrase comes from a passage in the New Testament of the Bible, James 2:14-26, where the writer James argues that faith without works is meaningless.

James begins by posing a hypothetical situation: what good is it if someone claims to have faith, but does not have any good deeds to show for it? Can such faith save them? James answers his own question by stating that faith by itself, without action, is dead. He goes on to give an example of how faith and works are interdependent, comparing faith without works to a body without a spirit. Just as a body without a spirit is lifeless, so too is faith without works.

The idea of faith without works being dead can be difficult to understand for some Christians. Some may argue that salvation comes through faith alone, and that good works are not necessary for salvation. However, James is not saying that good works are necessary for salvation. Rather, he is saying that good works are a natural outflow of genuine faith. If one truly believes in God and His teachings, that belief should lead to actions that reflect that faith.

James goes on to give several examples of how faith and works go hand in hand. He uses Abraham as an example, pointing out that Abraham's faith was made complete by his actions. Abraham's willingness to offer his son Isaac as a sacrifice demonstrated his faith in God, and his obedience to God's command showed that his faith was genuine.

Similarly, James uses the example of Rahab, a prostitute who helped the Israelites when they entered Jericho. Rahab's faith in God led her to protect the Israelite spies, even at great personal risk. Her actions demonstrated her faith in God, and as a result, she was saved.

James concludes by stating that just as the body is made alive by the spirit, so too is faith made alive by good works.

He argues that faith without works is useless, and that true faith is demonstrated through actions.

In summary, the phrase "faith without works is dead" emphasizes the importance of living out one's faith through good works. While good works are not necessary for salvation, they are a natural outflow of genuine faith. The examples of Abraham and Rahab demonstrate how faith and works go hand in hand, and how actions can demonstrate the genuineness of one's faith. As Christians, we are called not only to believe in God, but to live out our faith through actions that reflect that belief.

Faith is a deeply personal and complex aspect of human experience and accessing it can be a challenging and multifaceted process. However, with time and practice, anyone can learn to connect with their faith and cultivate a deeper sense of meaning and purpose in their lives.

7 Practical Steps to Access your Faith

Here are some practical steps you can take to access your faith:

1. Take time to reflect on your beliefs: Before you can access your faith, it's essential to understand what you believe and why. Spend time reflecting on your values, your understanding of the world, and your relationship with a higher power, if you have one. Journaling, meditation, and prayer are all effective tools for exploring your beliefs and deepening your understanding of them.
2. Connect with your community: Faith is often experienced within the context of a community. Connecting with other people who share your beliefs can be an excellent way to access your faith and feel supported in your spiritual journey.

Attend religious services, join a faith-based group, or seek out online communities where you can connect with like-minded individuals.

3. Practice gratitude: Cultivating a sense of gratitude can be a powerful way to connect with your faith. Take time each day to reflect on the blessings in your life and express gratitude for them. You might keep a gratitude journal, say a prayer of thanks, or simply take a few moments to appreciate the beauty around you.
4. Engage in acts of service: Many faiths emphasize the importance of service to others to connect with a higher power and live out one's values. Engaging in acts of service can be a powerful way to access your faith and feel a sense of purpose in your life. Volunteer at a local charity, help a friend in need, or simply practice kindness and compassion in your daily interactions.
5. Seek out spiritual practices: Engaging in spiritual practices can be an effective way to access your faith and cultivate a deeper sense of connection to a higher power. Depending on your beliefs, this might include prayer, meditation, chanting, or ritual. Experiment with different practices and find what resonates with you.
6. Practice self-care: Taking care of yourself is an essential part of accessing your faith. Make sure to prioritize your physical, emotional, and spiritual well-being. This might include regular exercise, getting enough sleep, spending time in nature, or engaging in activities that bring you joy.

7. Be open to growth and change: Accessing your faith is a journey, and it's important to remain open to growth and change along the way. Be willing to explore new ideas, challenge your beliefs, and seek out new experiences that can deepen your connection to a higher power.

Ephesians 3:20

Now unto him who is able to do exceedingly and abundantly above all we can ever ask or think according to the power that worketh in us.

God has already given us everything that we need ...

Philippians 4:13

Accessing your faith is a deeply personal and complex process, but by taking the time to reflect on your beliefs, connect with your community, practice gratitude, engage in acts of service, seek out spiritual practices, practice self-care, and remain open to growth and change, you can cultivate a deeper sense of meaning and purpose in your life.

Throughout history, faith has been a source of comfort and strength for individuals facing adversity and hardship. Whether it is the loss of a loved one, a personal crisis, or a global catastrophe, faith has provided solace and hope to those who have been touched by tragedy.

In this book, we will explore the power of faith and its impact on human life. We will examine the different forms that faith takes, from traditional religious belief to more contemporary expressions of spirituality. We will also look at the ways in which faith has been a driving force behind social and political movements, and how it has shaped the course of human history.

Through personal stories, historical anecdotes, and insights from leading scholars and thinkers, we will explore the ways in which faith can transform our lives and the world around us. Whether you are a person of faith, a skeptic, or simply curious about the power of belief, this book will offer insights and inspiration to help you explore the deeper questions of existence and the role that faith can play in our lives.

1

UNDERSTANDING FAITH

In this chapter, we will explore the concept of faith and its role in our lives. We will look at different definitions of faith, its benefits, and the barriers that can prevent us from accessing it.

Faith is a complex concept that is often difficult to define and understand. It can be described as a belief or trust in something or someone, often without any empirical evidence or proof. This can refer to a belief in a higher power, a religious doctrine, or a personal philosophy. Understanding faith requires exploring its various dimensions and considering its implications for individuals and society.

One of the key aspects of faith is its subjective nature. People's beliefs and experiences of faith can vary widely, depending on their personal history, culture, and worldview. For some, faith may be a source of comfort and meaning, while for others it may be a source of conflict and confusion. At the same time, faith can also have objective dimensions, as it can involve certain rituals, practices, and doctrines that are shared by a community of believers.

Religious faith is one of the most common forms of faith, and it is often associated with the belief in a transcendent reality or a divine being. This can take many different forms, ranging from monotheistic religions such as Christianity, Islam, and Judaism to polytheistic religions such as Hinduism and Shintoism. These religions often have a set of core beliefs and practices that are shared by their followers, and they can play an important role in shaping people's values, morals, and sense of identity.

However, faith is not limited to religious beliefs. People can also have faith in secular ideologies, such as democracy, human rights, and environmentalism. These beliefs may not have a supernatural or transcendent aspect, but they can still inspire people to act in certain ways and to strive for certain goals. In some cases, faith in secular ideologies can even take on a quasi-religious character, as people may form communities and engage in rituals and practices that reflect their shared beliefs.

Regardless of its form, faith can have important implications for individuals and society. On a personal level, faith can provide a sense of meaning, purpose, and direction, and it can help people cope with difficult situations and find a sense of peace and contentment. At the same time, faith can also be a source of conflict and division, as different beliefs and practices can lead to misunderstandings, intolerance, and even violence.

To truly understand faith, it is important to approach it with an open mind and a willingness to explore different perspectives. This may involve engaging in dialogue with people of different faiths and backgrounds, reading religious texts and philosophical works, and reflecting on one's own beliefs and experiences. By doing so, we can gain a deeper appreciation of the complex and multifaceted nature of faith, and we can work towards fostering greater understanding and respect among people of different faiths and cultures.

2

BUILDING YOUR FAITH

Practical ways to build your faith will be essential. Let's discuss the importance of prayer, meditation, and self-reflection, and provide tips for cultivating a positive mindset and a sense of gratitude. Building Your Faith: A Guide to Strengthening Your Belief. Faith is a powerful force that can help guide us through life's challenges and uncertainties. Whether you are religious or spiritual, developing your faith can help you find meaning and purpose in your life. Building your faith is a process that requires time, effort, and a willingness to explore your beliefs.

Here are some steps you can take to strengthen your faith.

1. Define Your Beliefs

The first step in building your faith is to define what you believe. Take some time to reflect on your beliefs, values, and experiences. Write them down and explore what they mean to you. Consider the teachings of your faith tradition, as well as your own personal experiences and insights. Clarifying your beliefs will help you stay grounded in your faith and provide a foundation for growth.

2. Engage with Your Community

No matter what your faith tradition, engaging with a community can be a powerful way to build your faith. Joining a religious or spiritual group can provide you with opportunities to learn from others, share your beliefs, and develop a sense of connection and belonging. Attend services, participate in discussions, and volunteer your time to build relationships with others who share your faith.

3. Study Your Tradition

Learning about your faith tradition can deepen your understanding and help you grow in your beliefs. Study the texts, teachings, and practices of your tradition. Take classes, read books, and attend workshops to deepen your knowledge. Consider seeking guidance from a mentor or spiritual leader who can help guide you on your journey.

4. Practice Your Beliefs

Putting your beliefs into practice is a crucial step in building your faith. Find ways to incorporate your beliefs into your daily life. Pray, meditate, or engage in other spiritual practices that help you connect with your faith. Act on your beliefs by volunteering, donating to charity, or helping those in need. By living your faith, you will deepen your connection to your beliefs.

5. Cultivate a Sense of Gratitude

Gratitude is an essential part of building your faith. Taking time to appreciate the blessings in your life can help you develop a sense of awe and wonder. Cultivate a habit of gratitude by keeping a journal, saying prayers of thanks, or simply taking time to reflect on the good things in your life. By focusing on the positive, you can develop a sense of joy and fulfillment that will strengthen your faith.

6. Embrace the Unknown

Faith requires a willingness to embrace the unknown. There will always be questions and uncertainties in life, and it is important to be open to exploring them. Rather than fearing the unknown, approach it with curiosity and a sense of adventure. Ask questions, seek answers, and be willing to challenge your beliefs. By embracing the unknown, you can deepen your understanding of your faith and develop a greater sense of trust in the universe.

Building your faith is a lifelong journey that requires patience, dedication, and a willingness to grow. By clarifying your beliefs, engaging with your community, studying your tradition, practicing your beliefs, cultivating gratitude, and embracing the unknown, you can strengthen your faith and find deeper meaning and purpose in your life.

3

OVERCOMING DOUBT

Doubt is a common barrier to accessing faith. In this chapter, we will explore the different types of doubt and provide strategies for overcoming them. We will discuss the role of evidence, logic, and personal experience in addressing doubt. Doubt is a natural human emotion that arises from uncertainty, fear, or lack of confidence. It is a feeling that can be crippling and can prevent people from achieving their goals and aspirations. Doubt can be paralyzing, causing people to second-guess their decisions and actions, and ultimately leading to inaction. However, it is possible to overcome doubt and move forward with confidence. In this chapter, we will explore some techniques that can help you overcome doubt.

1. Identify the source of your doubt.

To overcome doubt, it is important to identify its source. What is causing you to doubt yourself or your abilities? Is it fear of failure, lack of confidence, or a past experience that has left you feeling uncertain? By understanding the source of your doubt, you can begin to address it and find ways to overcome it.

2. Challenge your beliefs.

Doubt often arises from negative self-talk and limiting beliefs. To overcome doubt, it is important to challenge these beliefs and replace them with more positive and empowering ones. Ask yourself questions like, "Is this belief really true?" or "What evidence do I have to support this belief?" By questioning your beliefs, you can begin to break down the barriers that are holding you back.

3. Practice self-compassion

It is important to be kind and compassionate towards yourself when you are experiencing doubt. Treat yourself as you would treat a friend who is going through a difficult time. Remind yourself that doubt is a natural emotion and that it is okay to make mistakes. By practicing self-compassion, you can build your self-confidence and overcome doubt.

4. Take small steps

When you are feeling doubtful, it can be tempting to avoid taking action altogether. However, this only reinforces your doubt and makes it more difficult to overcome. Instead, take small steps towards your goal. Break down your goal into smaller, more manageable tasks and focus on completing them one by one. This will help you build momentum and increase your confidence.

5. Surround yourself with positive influences.

Surrounding yourself with positive and supportive people can help you overcome doubt. Seek out friends, family members, or mentors who can provide encouragement and support. Joining a group or community of like-minded individuals can also be helpful in building your confidence and overcoming doubt.

6. Practice mindfulness

Mindfulness is the practice of being present in the

moment and non-judgmentally observing your thoughts and emotions. Practicing mindfulness can help you overcome doubt by allowing you to observe your doubts without judgment or attachment. By observing your doubts in this way, you can begin to see them for what they are – temporary thoughts and emotions that do not define you. Doubt is a natural human emotion, but it does not have to hold you back. By identifying the source of your doubt, challenging your beliefs, practicing self-compassion, taking small steps, surrounding yourself with positive influences, and practicing mindfulness, you can overcome doubt and move forward with confidence. Remember, doubt is not a reflection of your abilities or worth. It is simply a passing emotion that can be overcome with persistence and self-care.

4

FINDING INSPIRATION

In this chapter, we will explore different sources of inspiration that can help you access your faith. We will discuss the role of community, mentors, and role models, and provide tips for finding inspiration in nature, art, and literature. Inspiration is the fuel that drives creativity. It is the spark that ignites the imagination and leads to innovative ideas. However, finding inspiration can be a daunting task, especially when creativity seems to have dried up.

Whether you are an artist, writer, musician, or anyone who relies on creativity to thrive, here are some tips on finding inspiration when you need it the most.

1. Explore the world around you.

Sometimes, all it takes is a change of scenery to find inspiration. Go for a walk in nature, visit a museum, or explore a new neighborhood. Pay attention to the details and let your senses be your guide. Take pictures, write down notes, or sketch what you see. You never know what might spark your creativity.

2. Try something new.

Trying new things can be a great way to find inspiration. Take a dance class, learn a new language, or try a new hobby. Getting out of your comfort zone can help you see things from a different perspective and give you a fresh take on old ideas.

3. Read, watch, and listen.

Books, movies, and music can be a great source of inspiration. Read a book in a different genre than you normally would, watch a movie that challenges your perspective, or listen to music from a different culture. Pay attention to the themes, characters, and storylines. You might find inspiration in the most unexpected places.

4. Collaborate

Collaborating with others can be a great way to find inspiration. Join a creative community, work with a partner, or bounce ideas off of friends. Collaboration can help you see things from different angles and provide fresh perspectives on your work.

5. Take a break.

Sometimes, the best way to find inspiration is to take a break. Step away from your work and do something completely unrelated. Take a nap, go for a run, or take a day off. Giving your brain a break can help you come back to your work with fresh eyes and renewed inspiration.

6. Keep a journal.

Keeping a journal can be a great way to capture ideas and inspiration. Write down your thoughts, dreams, and ideas as they come to you. You never know when a seemingly insignificant thought might lead to a great idea.

7. Embrace failure.

Finally, it is important to remember that failure is a natural part of the creative process. Embrace your failures and use them as a learning opportunity. Sometimes, the greatest inspiration can come from the most unexpected failures.

In conclusion, finding inspiration is not always easy, but it is essential to the creative process. By exploring the world around you, trying new things, reading, watching, and listening, collaborating, taking a break, keeping a journal, and embracing failure, you can find the inspiration you need to create your best work.

5

LIVING IN FAITH

Now we will explore practical ways to live in faith. We will discuss the importance of putting your beliefs into action, and provide tips for finding purpose and meaning in your life. We will also discuss the role of forgiveness and compassion in accessing your faith-Living in faith can be a fulfilling and rewarding experience, but it can also be a challenging one. Faith requires dedication, perseverance, and a willingness to trust in something beyond ourselves. In this chapter, we will explore some practical ways to live in faith that can help you develop and strengthen your spiritual journey.

1. Develop a daily spiritual practice: A daily spiritual practice can be anything that helps you connect with your faith. This could be prayer, meditation, reading religious texts, or attending religious services. By committing to a daily practice, you can create a space for yourself to reflect on your faith, build a deeper relationship

with your beliefs, and feel more grounded in your spiritual journey.

2. Surround yourself with a supportive community: Surrounding yourself with like-minded individuals who share your faith can provide you with a supportive community that can help you grow and develop your spiritual journey. Joining a faith-based group, attending religious services, or participating in online forums can help you connect with others who share your beliefs and provide a sense of community and belonging.
3. Practice gratitude: Practicing gratitude can be a powerful way to deepen your faith and cultivate a positive mindset. Take time each day to reflect on the blessings in your life, and express gratitude for the people, experiences, and opportunities that have helped shape who you are.
4. Serve others: Serving others is an important aspect of many faith traditions and can be a powerful way to live out your faith in practical ways. Look for opportunities to serve in your community, volunteer at a local charity, or find ways to support those in need. By serving others, you can help make a positive difference in the world and live out your faith in meaningful ways.
5. Embrace uncertainty: Living in faith can be a journey of ups and downs, and it's important to embrace the uncertainty that comes with it. Faith requires trust in something beyond ourselves, and that can be challenging at times. However, by embracing uncertainty and trusting in the journey, you can develop a deeper sense of faith and resilience in the face of challenges.

6. Seek guidance: Seeking guidance from a trusted spiritual advisor or mentor can be a valuable way to deepen your faith and gain insight into your spiritual journey. Consider reaching out to a religious leader, counselor, or mentor who can offer guidance, support, and encouragement as you navigate your faith journey.

Living in faith is a journey that requires dedication, perseverance, and a willingness to trust in something beyond ourselves. By developing a daily spiritual practice, surrounding yourself with a supportive community, practicing gratitude, serving others, embracing uncertainty, and seeking guidance, you can deepen your faith and experience the many rewards that come with a life lived in faith.

6

MAINTAINING YOUR FAITH

Maintaining your faith requires ongoing effort and attention. In this chapter, we will provide tips for staying connected to your faith, even in difficult times. We will discuss the importance of self-care, the role of rituals and traditions, and provide strategies for dealing with setbacks and challenges. Maintaining your faith can be a challenging task, especially when you are faced with adversity, doubt, or uncertainty. However, it is crucial to stay steadfast in your beliefs and continue to nurture your faith. Here are some tips on how to maintain your faith:

1. Keep a daily practice: It is essential to establish a daily practice that connects you with your faith. This could include prayer, meditation, or reading religious texts. By doing this every day, you are reminding yourself of your beliefs and strengthening your connection with your faith.
2. Surround yourself with like-minded individuals: Surrounding yourself with people who share

your beliefs can be helpful in maintaining your faith. Being a part of a community that supports your faith can provide you with the encouragement and motivation you need to stay strong.

3. Seek guidance: If you are struggling with doubt or uncertainty, seeking guidance from a trusted religious leader or mentor can help you clarify your beliefs and strengthen your faith.
4. Reflect on your experiences: Reflecting on past experiences where your faith has helped you overcome challenges can be a powerful way to maintain your faith. Remembering the times when your faith has been a source of strength and comfort can help you remain confident in your beliefs.
5. Practice forgiveness: Holding onto grudges or resentments can create negative energy that can weigh you down spiritually. Practicing forgiveness can help you let go of negative emotions and maintain a positive outlook on life.
6. Stay open-minded: It's important to stay open-minded and receptive to new ideas and perspectives. This doesn't mean you have to compromise your beliefs, but it does mean being willing to consider alternative viewpoints and learning from others.
7. Practice gratitude: Practicing gratitude can help you maintain your faith by reminding you of the good things in your life. Take time each day to reflect on what you are thankful for, and acknowledge the blessings that come your way.

In conclusion, maintaining your faith requires effort, commitment, and dedication. By following these tips, you can stay grounded in your beliefs and navigate through any challenges that come your way. Remember, your faith is a powerful source of strength and comfort, and by nurturing it, you can lead a fulfilling and meaningful life. Accessing your faith is a journey, and it requires effort and commitment. But with the right tools and strategies, you can tap into your inner strength and live a fulfilling and joyful life. Whether you are facing doubts or struggles, this book will provide you with the guidance and inspiration you need to access your faith and achieve your goals. Remember, you can do it!

7

FINDING HAPPINESS

Happiness is a joy produced by our emotions. People measure happiness consciously and subconsciously daily without even thinking. We can determine if someone is angry, sad, happy, depressed, frustrated, or hurt by just listening. The sound of their voice, tone, expressions, and gestures demonstrate emotions. Our behavior influences us feelings of happiness greatly which can be both enlightening and frustrating. For example, you tell yourself you can do it, push to succeed eventually you can reach a goal versus telling yourself you can't do it, never trying or ever reaching potential success. Words are power, you are what you say you are! Life's obstacles have forced me to be happy. My life hasn't always given me happiness. Good times, bad times, trials, and tribulations have taught me to be grateful for the things I have. The most valuable thing we have is time and it is not our own. God created us to give him praise for his enjoyment. It is impossible to praise God angry, mad, depressed, or frustrated. The spirit of the Lord is joyous, and he can turn any situation instantly. Every day is an opportunity to rejoice and be happy. We shouldn't worry but trust in our father who can do anything but fail. The two questionnaires produced similar results for me. According to my survey results I'm a very happy person which I absolutely agree with, life is too short to be unhappy.

The advantages and disadvantages of each questionnaire are extremely different; however, both questionnaires produced similar results. The advantage of the "Subjective Happiness scale" is it's short to the point with questions that make you think while being able to respond quickly to each question. The disadvantage to this questionnaire limits how much you learn about the person individually. The advantage of the "Oxford Happiness "questionnaire is that his personal information is obtained through this survey. The "Oxford Happiness" questionnaire gains a personal response versus the "Subjective Happiness Scale" questionnaire that gains a general response. The disadvantage of the "Oxford Happiness" questionnaire is length and thinking questions, this can be annoying or frustrating after a while. This questionnaire has twenty-nine questions compared to the "Subjective Happiness Scale" simple five questionnaire that delivers the same results.

The questions in the "Subjective Happiness scale" survey are general perspective questions. The "Oxford Happiness" survey are more personal questions. Each survey requires you to think and ask yourself if you're happy repeatedly in different forms. This forces us to think, observe and ask ourselves are we happy and why? According to my survey results these researchers successfully quantify the difficult and complex emotion of happiness. The results of both surveys are similar in my case. The "Subjective Happiness scale" survey I scored a seven defining me as a very happy person. The "Oxford Happiness" survey I scored a five equal to being very happy. I believe happiness can be measured. Happiness is created within it is a joy knowing one or thing can give or take away from you. You are what you say you are! Be Happy.

Happiness is a state of being that most of us strive to achieve in our lives. It is a feeling of contentment, satisfaction, and joy that we experience when we are fulfilled in different aspects of our lives, such as our relationships, careers, and personal growth. However, finding happiness can be challenging for many individuals, as it requires a combination of different factors, including self-awareness, self-care, and positive habits. In this chapter, we will explore some effective ways to find happiness in our lives.

- Cultivate Positive Relationships

One of the fundamental aspects of finding happiness is having positive relationships in our lives. Whether it's with family, friends, or romantic partners, relationships can significantly impact our happiness and well-being. Therefore, it is essential to surround ourselves with people who support us, respect us, and bring positivity into our lives.

Moreover, building and maintaining healthy relationships requires effort, empathy, and effective communication. We need to listen actively, express ourselves honestly, and understand each other's perspectives. By cultivating positive relationships, we create a sense of belonging, love, and connection that can enhance our happiness and overall quality of life.

- Practice Gratitude

Gratitude is a powerful tool for finding happiness. It is

the practice of being thankful and appreciative of the blessings in our lives, such as our health, relationships, accomplishments, and experiences. By focusing on what we have rather than what we lack, we can cultivate a positive mindset that can improve our well-being and happiness.

Practicing gratitude can be done in different ways, such as keeping a gratitude journal, expressing gratitude to others, or reflecting on what we are thankful for at the end of each day. By making gratitude a habit, we can train our brains to focus on the positive aspects of our lives and reduce stress, anxiety, and depression.

- Engage in Meaningful Activities

Engaging in activities that align with our values, interests, and passions can bring us happiness and fulfillment. Meaningful activities can vary from person to person, but they often involve personal growth, learning, creativity, and contributing to the greater good. By engaging in activities that give us a sense of purpose and meaning, we can increase our well-being and happiness.

For example, volunteering, pursuing a hobby, or learning a new skill can bring us joy and satisfaction. Moreover, engaging in activities with others can enhance our social connections and bring a sense of belonging and community.

- Practice Self-Care

Self-care is essential for finding happiness and well-being. It is the practice of taking care of ourselves physically, emotionally, and mentally. Self-care can include activities such as exercise, healthy eating, getting enough sleep, spending time in nature, and practicing mindfulness or meditation.

Moreover, practicing self-compassion and self-acceptance can improve our self-esteem and reduce stress and anxiety. By prioritizing our self-care, we can enhance our well-being and happiness, and have more energy and resilience to cope with life's challenges.

- Embrace Positive Habits

Positive habits can significantly impact our happiness and well-being. Habits are the repeated behaviors that shape our daily lives, and they can be either positive or negative. Positive habits can include activities such as practicing gratitude, engaging in meaningful activities, exercising regularly, and connecting with loved ones.

By embracing positive habits, we create a sense of structure and routine in our lives, which can reduce stress and anxiety. Moreover, positive habits can create a sense of accomplishment and satisfaction, which can enhance our happiness and overall well-being.

Finding happiness is a journey that requires effort, self-awareness, and effective habits. By cultivating positive relationships, practicing gratitude, engaging in meaningful activities, practicing self-care, and embracing positive habits.

8

LIFE IS GOOD

Do you have a good life? And if not, how do you get there? Meta - Ethics philosophy can help you seek and see the truth. I believe this is very important to understand due to our current state of emergency. Our nation's homelessness and drug epidemic are out of control. We walk by each other daily without speaking to one another or lending a helping hand, causing this generation to live hopeless and in fear not trusting anyone. Let's look at the ancient period's approach to "The Good" and "What is a good life". Socrates was the first to separate questions of Ethics / Morals from religion. He called this the "Socratic Turn". Socrates was a social critic and an actual legend. He challenged people to become investigators and critical thinkers. He would stop wherever he was in deep thought too just stop and think.

He believed in the Golden Rule as we all know it or should know. "treat people the way you want to be treated." Seems easy enough, right? Socrates' quote and his main question was "so how do you know that a particular act is God pleasing or not?" Socrates was on trial for corrupting young people. Most were afraid that the young people would pick up Socrates' nature. As a woman of faith, I believe God has a way of using you and your situation to get you where he wants you to be. Not to mention he has a wonderful sense of humor.

God created us to give him praise. He desires our praise which is pleasing to God. Which brings me to a word called Piety! Piety is another Dialectic Method Euthyphro demonstrates concern and an excellent example. Now while holiness song, dance, devotion to God is doing what God wants - his will. These terms make several assumptions on several levels when understanding Euthyphro. Euthyphro was a priest on trial trying his father on trial. Does God exist? Does God care about us? Well, if God cares, then it's his will. He used these terms and thoughts in search of truth while in court on trial.

Socrates, would have to question and think in thought of this "how little does the common hero know of the nature of the right and truth." His point was, what is good and what is not? Euthyphro on the other hand states piety is "looking after the Gods." He also states piety is "an art of sacrifice and prayer." In other words, when worshiping on one accord in spirit and truth, sacrificing to God, we demonstrate piety. I believe both were utilizing the will of God, to be pleasing to God knowing in truth and worship that God would be pleased by the praises of the righteousness so he can be lifted. God wants to use us for his enjoyment. So, we should speak to things as though they are and believe God's will will be done.

Genesis 1:1-5 God said, "Let there be light" and there was light. I am a firm believer that God exists and wants us to do good. The nature of the good meta - ethics according to Socrates good and evil are opposites. The Socratic turn helps demonstrate these beliefs and ensure God's faithfulness.

Religion can be a very sensitive subject and requires discussions to seek the truth and facts of our Lord and Savior God. We can argue, agree, or disagree but until we come to a common ground and "logical" thoughts. Comprehension moving forward or interpretation of the word giving a different meaning and gestures will constantly affect us. Just saying hello to someone can change their day and outlook on life. Having the activities of our limbs being sane in our right frame of mind is a blessing and joy too. Sometimes we say things without meaning to hurt someone's feelings intentionally, I believe the hardest thing is being honest with yourself. This will cause you to self-examine yourself and create a relationship with our father.

Doing his will comes naturally and should manifest hourly good in all you do. Be happy! The direction of Socrates and Euthyphro in court demonstrates "good will" and the will to do good. The Socratic Turn is why the ancient Greeks decided that reason should be the bar and decided to adopt the belief and support the Socratic Turn. Living a good life is a universal goal that many people aspire to. However, what it means to live a good life can differ from person to person. Some may see it as having a successful career, while others may prioritize having strong relationships and being happy. Regardless of the specifics, there are certain principles that can guide us towards living a good life.

One of the most important principles is to cultivate a sense of purpose. Having a clear idea of what we want to accomplish in life can give us direction and motivation. This purpose could be related to our work, our relationships, or something else entirely. It's important to reflect on our values and passions to identify what truly drives us.

Another key aspect of living a good life is to prioritize our physical and mental health. This means taking care of our bodies through regular exercise, healthy eating habits, and sufficient sleep. It also means prioritizing our mental health by practicing self-care, seeking support when needed, and engaging in activities that promote well-being, such as meditation or hobbies we enjoy.

In addition to taking care of ourselves, it's important to cultivate strong relationships with others. This means investing time and energy into building and maintaining relationships with family, friends, and other important people in our lives. We can do this by practicing active listening, being supportive, and making time for regular connection.

Another principle that can help us live a good life is to prioritize personal growth and learning. This can involve pursuing educational opportunities, engaging in hobbies or interests, and challenging ourselves to step outside of our comfort zones. By continually learning and growing, we can gain new perspectives and skills that can enrich our lives and help us achieve our goals.

Living a good life also involves being mindful of our impact on the world around us. This means being responsible and ethical in our actions and choices, and making an effort to contribute positively to our communities and the environment.

Finally, it's important to cultivate gratitude and appreciation for what we have. This means focusing on the good things in our lives and expressing gratitude for them regularly. By cultivating a positive mindset and focusing on the good, we can increase our overall sense of happiness and fulfillment.

Remember, living a good life involves cultivating a sense of purpose, prioritizing our health and well-being, nurturing strong relationships, prioritizing personal growth and learning, being mindful of our impact on the world, and cultivating gratitude and appreciation. By focusing on these principles, we can build a life that is meaningful, fulfilling, and rewarding.

9

WHO AM I?

Let's explore the concept of being a child of the Most High God. We will examine what it means to be a child of God, who we are as children of God, and how our identity as God's children shapes our lives. We will also look at the ways in which our relationship with God can be strengthened and deepened, and how we can live out our identity as God's children in the world.

Who is God? To understand who we are as children of God, we must first understand who God is. In this chapter, we will explore the nature of God, his attributes, and how he has revealed himself to us through the Bible. We will look at the concept of the Trinity and how it affects our understanding of God, as well as the idea of God's sovereignty and how it relates to our lives. The concept of God has been a subject of debate and discussion for thousands of years. In different cultures and religions, the idea of God varies, and there are many different interpretations of who God is. However, there are some commonalities in many beliefs, and in this chapter, we will explore some of the most common conceptions of God.

God is the creator of the universe. He is alpha and omega, the beginning and the end. God is the ultimate power that brought everything into being. God is responsible for the existence of the universe and all that is in it. God is omnipotent, meaning that God is all-powerful. This means that there is nothing that God cannot do. This means that God can perform miracles or intervene in the course of events on Earth. God is omniscient, meaning that God is all-knowing. This means that God knows everything that has happened, is happening, and will happen. God has a plan for the universe and everything in it, and that everything happens for a reason.

God is benevolent, meaning that God is all-loving and compassionate. This means that God cares for every living being and wants what is best for them. This means that God answers prayers and provides guidance to people who seek it. Ultimately, God provides a source of comfort, guidance, and hope in the face of life's challenges..

10

WHAT DOES IT MEAN TO BE A CHILD OF GOD?

When we accept Christ as our personal Savior we become a child of God. This separates us from others and protects us from all hurt and harm Learning and knowing what it means to be a child of God. We will look at the biblical basis for this concept, and how it is expressed in the New Testament. We will also examine how being a child of God relates to our salvation and our relationship with God. Being a child of God is a spiritual concept that is found in many religious traditions. It refers to the idea that through faith and belief in God, an individual becomes a member of God's family, and enjoys certain benefits and blessings. Eternal life is one of many benefits of being a child of God.

- Eternal Life: One of the most significant benefits of being a child of God is the promise of eternal life. For those who believe in God and accept Jesus Christ as their savior, death is not the end. Instead, it is a transition to a new life in heaven, where there is no pain, suffering, or death.

- Forgiveness: Another benefit of being a child of God is forgiveness. God is a loving and forgiving God, and He offers forgiveness to those who repent of their sins and turn to Him. As a child of God, you can have the assurance that your sins are forgiven, and you can have a fresh start.
- Peace: Being a child of God also brings peace. In a world that is filled with chaos and turmoil, having the peace that comes from knowing God and His love can be a source of great comfort. As Jesus said, "Peace I leave with you; my peace I give you. I do not give to you as the world gives. Do not let your hearts be troubled and do not be afraid." (John 14:27)
- Guidance: As a child of God, you have access to divine guidance. God's Word, the Bible, provides wisdom and direction for every aspect of life. When faced with difficult decisions or challenges, you can turn to God's Word for guidance and direction.
- Strength: God also provides strength to His children. When faced with trials and difficulties, we can turn to God for strength to endure and overcome. As the Apostle Paul wrote, "I can do all things through him who gives me strength." (Philippians 4:13)
- Hope: Being a child of God also brings hope. In a world that can sometimes seem hopeless, knowing that God is in control and that He has a plan for our lives can be a source of great hope and encouragement. As the Bible says, "For I know the plans I have for you," declares the Lord,

"plans to prosper you and not to harm you, plans to give you hope and a future." (Jeremiah 29:11)

- Love: Finally, being a child of God means experiencing the unconditional love of God. God's love is not based on our performance or our worthiness, but on His grace and mercy. As the Apostle John wrote, "See what great love the Father has lavished on us, that we should be called children of God! And that is what we are!" (1 John 3:1)

Being a child of God is a privilege and a blessing. It brings with it the promise of eternal life, forgiveness, peace, guidance, strength, hope, and love. If you have not yet experienced the benefits of being a child of God, I encourage you to seek Him and to place your faith and trust in Him.

11

OUR IDENTITY AS CHILDREN OF GOD

Let's look at our identity as children of God. We will examine the ways in which our identity is shaped by our relationship with God, and how it affects the way we see ourselves and the world around us. We will also explore the idea of spiritual adoption and how it relates to our identity as God's children.Our identity is shaped by a myriad of factors, including our upbringing, experiences, relationships, and beliefs. One of the most profound influences on our identity is our relationship with God. Whether we believe in God or not, our perception of a higher power and our interactions with it can significantly impact how we see ourselves and our place in the world.

For those who believe in God, their relationship with Him can be a source of strength, comfort, and guidance. They see themselves as children of God, created in His image and imbued with a purpose and destiny that is inextricably linked to their relationship with Him. Their identity is rooted in their faith, and their belief in God gives them a sense of belonging and connection to something greater than themselves.

The way we perceive God can also impact our identity. If we see God as a loving and compassionate parent, we may feel more secure and confident in our identity, knowing that we are loved unconditionally. However, if we view God as a punishing and judgmental figure, we may struggle with feelings of inadequacy, shame, and unworthiness.

Our relationship with God can also influence how we see ourselves in relation to others. For example, if we believe that God has called us to serve others, we may see ourselves as humble servants and strive to live a life of compassion and service. On the other hand, if we see ourselves as superior to others because of our faith, we may struggle with arrogance and a sense of entitlement.

For those who do not believe in God, their identity may still be shaped by their relationship with a higher power or a sense of purpose beyond themselves. They may see themselves as part of a larger community, connected to others by a shared sense of values or a common goal. Their identity may be shaped by their commitment to making the world a better place or by their desire to leave a positive legacy.

Ultimately, our relationship with God, or lack thereof, can shape our identity in profound ways. It can influence how we see ourselves, how we relate to others, and how we navigate the challenges and opportunities of life. Whether we believe in God or not, our relationship with a higher power or sense of purpose can provide us with a sense of meaning, purpose, and direction, and help us to become the best version of ourselves.

The concept of spiritual adoption is a key aspect of Christian theology and relates to our identity as God's children. It is rooted in the belief that through faith in Jesus Christ, believers are adopted into the family of God and receive all the benefits of being a child of God.

The idea of adoption was familiar in the culture of the ancient world, where it was seen as a legal process by which a childless couple could take on a child to become their heir. In the Roman world, adoption was often used as a way of securing an heir for wealthy families who were unable to have children.

In the New Testament, the concept of adoption is used to describe the relationship between God and believers. In Romans 8:15-16, the Apostle Paul writes, "For you did not receive a spirit of slavery to fall back into fear, but you have received a spirit of adoption. When we cry, 'Abba! Father!' it is that very Spirit bearing witness with our spirit that we are children of God."

Through faith in Jesus Christ, believers are adopted into God's family and receive the status of children. This adoption is not a legal or formal process, but a spiritual reality that is brought about through the work of the Holy Spirit. As children of God, believers are granted all the privileges of being part of God's family, including access to the Father, the love of God, and the promise of eternal life.

The concept of spiritual adoption has important implications for our understanding of our identity as Christians. By being adopted into God's family, we are given a new identity as children of God. This identity is not based on our own merit or worthiness but is bestowed upon us by God's grace.

As children of God, we are called to live in a way that reflects our new identity. This includes living a life of obedience to God, showing love to others, and pursuing holiness. It also means that we can have confidence in our relationship with God, knowing that we have been accepted and loved by Him.

In addition to our individual identity as children of God,

the concept of spiritual adoption also has implications for our understanding of the church as the family of God. As believers, we are all adopted into the same family, united by our common faith in Jesus Christ. This means that we are called to love and care for one another as brothers and sisters in Christ.

The idea of spiritual adoption is a key aspect of Christian theology that relates to our identity as God's children. Through faith in Jesus Christ, believers are adopted into God's family and given a new identity as children of God. This identity is not based on our own merit but is bestowed upon us by God's grace. As children of God, we are called to live in a way that reflects our new identity and to love and care for one another as members of the same family.

12

LIVING AS CHILDREN OF GOD

How our identity as children of God affects the way we live our lives. We will look at the fruit of the Spirit and how it should be evident in the lives of those who are God's children. We will also examine the idea of sanctification and how it relates to our ongoing transformation as children of God.As children of God, our identity is deeply rooted in our faith and relationship with Him. This identity shapes the way we perceive ourselves, the world around us, and ultimately how we live our lives. Here are some ways in which our identity as children of God affects the way we live. As children of God, we understand that our purpose in life is not solely to achieve success or accumulate wealth, but rather to serve and glorify God. This understanding brings meaning and fulfillment to our lives, as we strive to live in a way that honors Him and His teachings. We are reminded that our actions have a greater purpose and that we are part of something bigger than ourselves.

Our identity as children of God also shapes the way we

love and interact with others. We are called to love our neighbors as ourselves and to show compassion to those in need. This means that we are called to love others unconditionally, without discrimination or judgment, just as God loves us. This love extends beyond our family and friends to encompass all people, even those who may seem difficult to love.

As children of God, we are called to live according to His moral values. This means that we are called to live with integrity, honesty, and humility. We are also called to respect others, care for the environment, and seek justice for the oppressed. These values shape our character and influence the way we make decisions in our personal and Forgiveness and Grace

Our identity as children of God also teaches us the importance of forgiveness and grace. We understand that we are all sinners and in need of forgiveness, and that God extends His grace to us freely. This knowledge enables us to forgive others, even when it is difficult, and to extend grace to those who may have wronged us. This attitude of forgiveness and grace helps to foster healthy relationships and promotes reconciliation.

As children of God, we also have hope and trust in Him. We understand that even in the midst of difficulties and trials, God is with us and working for our good. This hope and trust enable us to face challenges with courage and to trust in God's plan for our lives. We are reminded that our ultimate hope is in heaven, and that we are called to live in a way that reflects this hope.

Our identity as children of God shapes the way we live our lives in significant ways. It gives us purpose, love, moral values, forgiveness, grace, hope, and trust. It enables us to live in a way that reflects God's love and to make a positive impact on the world around us. As we continue to grow in our faith and relationship with God, may we always remember our identity as His children and strive to live in a way that honors Him.

13

STRENGTHENING OUR RELATIONSHIP WITH GOD

We will explore ways in which we can strengthen our relationship with God. We will examine the importance of prayer, Bible study, and fellowship with other believers. We will also explore the concept of spiritual disciplines and how they can help us to grow in our faith. Strengthening our relationship with God is a journey that requires consistent effort and dedication. It involves taking deliberate steps to deepen our faith, grow spiritually and draw closer to our Creator. Here are some practical ways to strengthen our relationship with God. Prayer is a powerful tool for communicating with God. It allows us to express our gratitude, share our concerns, seek guidance, and ask for forgiveness. Make it a habit to pray daily, not just when things are going wrong, but also when things are going well.

The Bible is the word of God, and it is the ultimate guide for living a life that is pleasing to God. Set aside time each day to read the Bible, and allow its teachings to transform your life.

Attending church provides an opportunity to worship God with other believers and to learn from others who are also seeking to grow in their faith. Find a church that aligns with your beliefs and make it a priority to attend regularly. Jesus taught that the greatest among us are those who serve others. Find ways to serve others, whether through volunteering, giving to charity, or helping those in need. Serving others not only blesses them but also helps us grow in our relationship with God. Fellowship with other believers can be a source of encouragement and support. Find a group of believers who share your values and beliefs, and make time to fellowship with them regularly.

Having gratitude is a key component of a healthy relationship with God. Take time each day to reflect on the blessings in your life, and express gratitude to God for them. This helps us develop a positive outlook on life and strengthens our faith. This is why trust is an essential element of any relationship, and our relationship with God is no exception. Trusting in God means believing that He has our best interests at heart, even when we don't understand His plan. Learn to trust in God's promises and rely on His strength. Our relationship with God is not just about what we say, but also about what we do. Live out your faith by being a positive influence in the world, treating others with kindness and respect, and living a life that is in alignment with God's teachings.

Strengthening our relationship with God requires intentional effort and consistent practice. By making prayer, Bible study, attending church, serving others, seeking fellowship, practicing gratitude, trusting in God, and living out our faith a regular part of our lives, we can draw closer to our Creator and experience the fullness of His love and grace.

Prayer is a practice that has been a part of human culture and tradition since time immemorial. It is a way of communicating with the divine, and expressing gratitude, hope, and faith. Prayer is not just a religious practice, but it is also a powerful tool that can have a positive impact on our physical, mental, and emotional well-being.

The Importance of Prayer

Prayer is an essential part of many religions, and it serves many purposes. It is a way of seeking guidance, expressing gratitude, asking for forgiveness, and seeking strength in times of difficulty. Prayer can be a source of comfort, hope, and inspiration for those who believe in a higher power.

For many people, prayer is a way of connecting with the divine and finding a sense of purpose and meaning in life. It can help individuals to focus on what is important and to gain perspective on their problems and challenges. Prayer can also provide a sense of community and belonging, as people come together to pray for a common cause.

Prayer and Physical Health

Studies have shown that prayer can have a positive impact on physical health. Regular prayer has been linked to lower blood pressure, reduced stress levels, and improved immune function. Prayer can also promote better sleep, and help individuals to cope with chronic pain and illness.

Prayer is a spiritual practice that has been utilized by people for centuries. It is often associated with religious beliefs, but it can also be a personal and private practice that is done for comfort and guidance. While prayer is primarily viewed as a spiritual activity, research has shown that it can also have a positive impact on physical health. In this chapter, we will explore how prayer can help improve physical health.

1. Reducing stress levels

Prayer has been found to be an effective stress reliever. When people pray, they enter a state of relaxation, which can help reduce stress levels. Prayer has been shown to reduce the levels of cortisol, which is a hormone that is released in response to stress. High levels of cortisol can lead to a range of health problems, including heart disease, obesity, and depression. By reducing stress levels, prayer can help reduce the risk of these health problems.

2. Boosting the immune system

Prayer has also been shown to boost the immune system. When people pray, they experience positive emotions, such as love, gratitude, and compassion. These positive emotions can lead to an increase in the production of white blood cells, which are essential for fighting off infections and diseases. By boosting the immune system, prayer can help prevent illnesses and infections.

3. Promoting healing

Prayer has been found to promote healing in the body. Research has shown that people who pray regularly experience faster recovery times after surgery or illness. Prayer can also help reduce pain levels and improve the overall sense of well-being. By promoting healing, prayer can help people recover from illnesses and injuries more quickly.

4. Lowering blood pressure

High blood pressure is a significant risk factor for heart

disease, stroke, and other health problems. Prayer has been found to lower blood pressure levels. When people pray, they enter a state of relaxation, which can help lower blood pressure. Prayer can also help reduce anxiety levels, which can contribute to high blood pressure.

5. Improving mental health

Prayer can also have a positive impact on mental health. When people pray, they experience feelings of peace, calm, and happiness. Prayer can help reduce anxiety and depression levels, which can contribute to a range of mental health problems. By improving mental health, prayer can help people lead happier, more fulfilling lives.

Prayer can have a significant impact on physical health. By reducing stress levels, boosting the immune system, promoting healing, lowering blood pressure, and improving mental health, prayer can help people lead healthier and happier lives. While prayer is often associated with religious beliefs, it can also be a personal and private practice that can be done by anyone, regardless of their beliefs. If you are interested in improving your physical health, consider incorporating prayer into your daily routine.

Prayer and Mental Health

In addition to its physical health benefits, prayer can also have a positive impact on mental health. Prayer can provide a sense of calm and inner peace, which can help to reduce anxiety and depression. Prayer can also provide a sense of hope and optimism, which can help individuals to cope with difficult situations and find meaning and purpose in their lives.

Prayer is a practice that has been a part of many cultures

and religions throughout human history. It involves communicating with a higher power or deity through words, thoughts, or actions. While the benefits of prayer are often associated with spiritual or religious beliefs, there is growing evidence that prayer can also have positive effects on mental health.

One of the primary attributes of prayer is its ability to reduce stress and anxiety. Prayer allows individuals to express their worries and concerns to a higher power, which can provide a sense of comfort and reassurance. Studies have shown that individuals who pray regularly are less likely to experience symptoms of depression and anxiety than those who do not pray.

Prayer also has the potential to improve mood and increase feelings of well-being. It has been found to release endorphins, which are the body's natural feel-good chemicals. This can result in feelings of relaxation, calmness, and happiness. Additionally, prayer can provide a sense of purpose and meaning, which is important for maintaining mental health.

Another attribute of prayer is its ability to foster a sense of connection and social support. Many religious traditions involve prayer as a communal activity, which allows individuals to come together and share their experiences and struggles. This can provide a sense of belonging and social support, which is important for mental health.

Prayer can also promote self-reflection and introspection. It allows individuals to examine their thoughts, emotions, and behaviors, which can lead to greater self-awareness and personal growth. This can help individuals to better understand themselves and their relationships with others, which can result in improved mental health and well-being.

Finally, prayer can provide a sense of hope and optimism. It allows individuals to focus on positive outcomes and possibilities, which can counteract feelings of hopelessness and despair. This can be particularly important for individuals who are dealing with chronic illness or other challenges that can negatively impact mental health.

Prayer can have a range of positive effects on mental health. It can reduce stress and anxiety, improve mood and well-being, foster social support and connection, promote self-reflection and personal growth, and provide a sense of hope and optimism. While the benefits of prayer are often associated with spiritual or religious beliefs, individuals from all backgrounds can potentially benefit from incorporating prayer into their daily routine.

Prayer and Spiritual Growth

Prayer can be a powerful tool for spiritual growth and development. It can help individuals to deepen their relationship with the divine and to develop a sense of inner peace and contentment. Prayer can also help individuals to develop greater compassion, forgiveness, and empathy towards others.

Prayer can be a deeply personal and meaningful practice, and it can be done in a variety of ways. Some people prefer to pray alone, while others prefer to pray in a group. Some people use prayer as a way of expressing gratitude, while others use it as a way of seeking guidance and support. Whatever the purpose or method, prayer can be a powerful tool for personal growth, healing, and transformation.

Prayer is an important practice that can have a positive impact on our physical, mental, and spiritual well-being. It is a way of connecting with the divine, expressing gratitude and hope, and finding inner peace and contentment. Whether we practice prayer as part of a religious tradition or as a personal practice, it can help us to lead happier, healthier, and more fulfilling lives.

Prayer is a deeply personal and transformative practice that has been part of human experience since the beginning of time. It is an act of communication with a higher power or divine being, often associated with a specific religion or belief system. Although the ways in which people pray may differ, the benefits of prayer for spiritual growth and development are universal.

At its core, prayer is a way to connect with something greater than ourselves. Whether it is a deity, a universal force, or a sense of inner peace, prayer helps us to transcend our individual experiences and connect with something larger. By focusing our attention and intention in prayer, we open ourselves up to new possibilities and experiences beyond our immediate circumstances.

Prayer can be a powerful tool for spiritual growth and development in several ways. Here are some of the key ways in which prayer can transform our lives:

1. Deepens our relationship with a higher power or divine being

Prayer is an opportunity to cultivate a deeper relationship with the divine. By regularly engaging in prayer, we develop a sense of familiarity and trust with the divine presence in our lives. We may come to see our prayers answered in unexpected ways, or feel a sense of comfort and guidance during difficult times. This sense of connection and intimacy can bring a sense of peace, purpose, and fulfillment to our lives.

2. Increases our sense of gratitude and appreciation

Prayer can help us to cultivate a spirit of gratitude and appreciation for the blessings in our lives. By taking time to express our thanks for the gifts we have received, we become more mindful of the abundance around us. This can shift our focus from what we lack to what we have, and increase our overall sense of happiness and contentment.

3. Provides a sense of inner peace and calm

Prayer can be a way to cultivate a sense of inner peace and calm. When we pray, we bring our attention to the present moment and focus on the divine presence within and around us. This can help us to release feelings of anxiety, stress, and fear, and cultivate a sense of trust and surrender to the divine plan.

4. Helps us to clarify our intentions and goals

Prayer can be a way to clarify our intentions and goals in life. By setting our intentions and desires in prayer, we bring them to the forefront of our awareness and invite the divine to support us in achieving them. This can help us to stay focused and motivated in pursuing our dreams, and align our actions with our values and beliefs.

5. Cultivates compassion and empathy

Prayer can help us to cultivate a sense of compassion and empathy for others. By praying for the well-being of others, we connect with their struggles and offer our support and love. This can deepen our sense of connection and belonging with others, and inspire us to act with kindness and generosity in the world.

Prayer changes things and is a powerful tool for spiritual growth and development that can bring a sense of connection, gratitude, peace, clarity, and compassion to our lives. Whether we practice prayer as part of a religious tradition or in our own unique way, the benefits of prayer are universal and accessible to all who seek them. By making prayer a regular part of our lives, we can transform ourselves and the world around us.

14

SHARING THE LOVE OF GOD WITH OTHERS

Let's examine how we can share the love of God with others. We will explore the concept of evangelism and how we can effectively communicate the gospel to those around us. We will also look at the idea of social justice and how we can work to bring about positive change in the world. Sharing the love of God with others is one of the most important responsibilities that Christians have. As believers, we are called to be the light of the world and to spread the love of God to those around us. This can be done in a variety of ways, and in this chapter, we will explore some of the most effective ways to share the love of God with others.

One of the most important things that we can do when sharing the love of God with others is to live a life that is reflective of God's love. This means that we must strive to live a life that is filled with compassion, kindness, and generosity. When people see us living our lives in this way, they will be drawn to the love that we have in our hearts, and they will be more open to hearing about the love of God.

Another effective way to share the love of God with others is to engage in acts of service. This could mean volunteering at a local soup kitchen, helping to build a home with Habitat for Humanity, or simply offering to mow a neighbor's lawn. When we engage in acts of service, we are showing people that we care about them and that we are willing to go out of our way to help them. This is a powerful way to demonstrate the love of God in action.

In addition to living a life of love and engaging in acts of service, we can also share the love of God through our words. This could mean sharing our personal testimony of how God has worked in our lives, or simply offering a word of encouragement to someone who is going through a difficult time. It's important to remember that sharing the love of God with others doesn't always have to involve a formal presentation or sermon. Sometimes, all it takes is a simple word of kindness to make a big impact.

Another way to share the love of God with others is to invite them to church. Church can be a powerful place to experience the love of God in community, and it's often easier for people to connect with God when they are surrounded by other believers. By inviting someone to church, we are not only showing them that we care about them, but we are also giving them the opportunity to experience the love of God in a powerful way.

Remember that one of the most important things that we can do when sharing the love of God with others is to pray for them. Prayer is a powerful tool that we can use to intercede on behalf of others and to ask God to work in their lives. When we pray for someone, we are demonstrating our love and concern for them, and we are inviting God to work in their hearts and lives.

Sharing the love of God with others is an essential part

of our faith as Christians. Whether we are living a life of love, engaging in acts of service, sharing our words, inviting people to church, or praying for others, there are many ways that we can demonstrate the love of God to those around us. By doing so, we can help to make the world a better place and bring others closer to the love of God.

We have explored what it means to be a child of the Most High God. We have looked at who God is, what it means to be a child of God, and how our identity as God's children shapes our lives. We have also examined ways in which we can strengthen our relationship with God and share his love with others. As we continue on our journey as children of God, may we always remember the great love that God has for us, and may we seek to live out our identity as his beloved children in all that we do.

15

FEAR IS NOT OF GOD

As Christians, our faith in God is the foundation of our lives. It shapes our thoughts, actions, and beliefs. One of the most important teachings of Christianity is to not live in fear. Fear can have a negative impact on our mental, emotional, and physical well-being. In this chapter, we will explore why as Christians we do not believe in fear, and how we can overcome it.

Fear is a powerful emotion that can cripple a person's life. It can prevent us from achieving our goals and living our lives to the fullest. Fear can be caused by a variety of factors, including past traumas, present circumstances, and future uncertainties. Regardless of the cause, fear is not of God.

In the Bible, fear is often described as a lack of faith. In Matthew 8:26, Jesus rebukes his disciples for their fear during a storm, saying, "Why are you afraid, O you of little faith?" Similarly, Paul writes in 2 Timothy 1:7, "For God gave us a spirit not of fear but of power and love and self-control."

God wants us to trust in him and not be consumed by fear. Fear is a tool that the devil uses to keep us from living our lives for God. The devil wants us to be paralyzed by fear so that we do not live out our purpose or share the gospel with others. However, God has not given us a spirit of fear, but rather one of power, love, and self-control.

When we face fear, we can turn to God for strength and courage. In Psalm 56:3-4, it is written, "When I am afraid, I put my trust in you. In God, whose word I praise, in God I trust; I shall not be afraid. What can flesh do to me?" This verse reminds us that we can find refuge in God and that he will protect us from our fears.

It is important to note that fear can be a natural response to dangerous situations. For example, if someone is in the presence of a threatening animal or person, fear can be a helpful response that allows them to take appropriate action. However, fear becomes a problem when it is irrational and prevents us from living our lives to the fullest.

Fear is not of God. Instead, God has given us a spirit of power, love, and self-control. When we face fear, we can turn to God for strength and courage. By trusting in God, we can overcome our fears and live our lives to the fullest.

Fear is a natural emotion that all humans experience at some point in their lives. Whether it's fear of the unknown, fear of failure, or fear of the future, it can be a paralyzing feeling that prevents us from living life to the fullest. However, it's important to know that fear can be overcome with the right mindset and tools. In this chapter, we will discuss some effective strategies for overcoming fear.

Identify your fear.

The first step to overcoming fear is to identify what it is that you are afraid of. This could be a specific situation, person, or event. Once you have identified your fear, it's important to understand why you are afraid. Is it because of a past experience, or is it because you have never encountered this situation before? Understanding the root cause of your fear can help you to develop a plan for overcoming it.

Face your fear.

One of the most effective ways to overcome fear is to face it head- on. This may seem daunting, but it's important to remember that fear is often worse in our minds than it is in reality. Start by taking small steps towards your fear. For example, if you are afraid of public speaking, start by speaking in front of a small group of people before working your way up to larger audiences. The more you face your fear, the less power it will have over you.

Practice relaxation techniques

Fear can be a stressful and overwhelming emotion. Learning relaxation techniques such as deep breathing, meditation, or yoga can help to reduce anxiety and calm your mind. When you feel fear starting to take over, take a few deep breaths and focus on your breathing. This can help to slow down your heart rate and bring a sense of calm.

Surround yourself with positivity

Surrounding yourself with positive people and influences can help to boost your confidence and reduce fear. Spend time with people who encourage and support you, and avoid those who bring you down. Positive affirmations and self-talk can also be helpful. Repeat positive affirmations to yourself, such as "I am strong" or "I can do this" to help build confidence.

Seek professional help

If your fear is particularly intense or is interfering with your daily life, it may be helpful to seek professional help. A therapist or counselor can work with you to identify the root cause of your fear and develop a plan for overcoming it. They may also teach you coping strategies and techniques for managing anxiety.

Fear is a natural emotion that everyone experiences at some point. However, it's important to know that fear can be overcome with the right mindset and tools. By identifying your fear, facing it head-on, practicing relaxation techniques, surrounding yourself with positivity, and seeking professional help if needed, you can overcome fear and live a fulfilling life.

16

THE POWER OF LOVE AND OF A SOUND MIND

Love and a sound mind are two powerful concepts that have the ability to transform individuals and the world at large. Love is a force that has been celebrated throughout history, and it has been described as a feeling of deep affection, a strong attachment or devotion, and an unselfish concern for the welfare of others. A sound mind, on the other hand, refers to a state of mental health and stability, where an individual can think clearly, make rational decisions, and manage their emotions effectively.

The Power of Love:

Love is a powerful emotion that has the ability to bring people together and to create a sense of unity and belonging. When we feel loved, we are more likely to be happy, healthy, and fulfilled. Love can also be a source of strength and inspiration, helping us to overcome challenges and to persevere through difficult times.

Love can take many forms, including romantic love, love for family and friends, and even love for strangers or for humanity as a whole. Love can inspire us to be kind, compassionate, and generous, and it can motivate us to make a positive difference in the world.

The Power of a Sound Mind:

A sound mind is essential for mental health and well-being. When our minds are healthy and balanced, we are better able to manage stress, make rational decisions, and maintain positive relationships with others. A sound mind is also important for achieving our goals and fulfilling our potential.

A sound mind can be cultivated through various practices, such as mindfulness, meditation, and therapy. These practices can help us to become more aware of our thoughts and emotions, and to develop greater emotional intelligence and resilience.

The Power of Love and a Sound Mind Combined:

When love and a sound mind are combined, they have the power to transform individuals and society as a whole. Love can inspire us to seek mental health and well-being, and a sound mind can help us to cultivate greater empathy, compassion, and kindness towards others.

When we have a sound mind and a loving heart, we are better equipped to navigate the challenges of life, to overcome adversity, and to create positive change in the world. We are more likely to treat others with respect, dignity, and kindness, and we are more likely to work towards a common goal of creating a more just and equitable society.

The power of love and of a sound mind cannot be overstated. These two concepts have the ability to transform individuals and to create a better world for all. By cultivating these qualities within ourselves and promoting them in our communities, we can create a more compassionate, connected, and thriving world.

The Bible tells us that fear is not from God. 2 Timothy 1:7

says, "For God has not given us a spirit of fear, but of power and of love and of a sound mind." Fear is a tool of the enemy, Satan, to paralyze us and prevent us from living the life that God has planned for us. When we believe in fear, we are not believing in God's power and love.

17

FAITH OVER FEAR

As Christians, we are called to have faith over fear. Hebrews 11:1 says, "Now faith is the substance of things hoped for, the evidence of things not seen." Faith is the opposite of fear. When we have faith in God, we trust that He is in control, and we do not need to fear. We can face any situation with confidence and courage, knowing that God is with us.

Faith Over Fear: Overcoming Life's Challenges

Life is full of challenges and uncertainties that can often lead to fear and anxiety. It's easy to get caught up in the worries of what might happen, but this only leads to more stress and negative thoughts. However, one of the most powerful tools we have to overcome fear is faith.

Faith is a belief in something greater than ourselves, whether that be a higher power, the universe, or even our own inner strength. It is a source of hope, comfort, and guidance that can help us navigate through life's challenges with confidence and resilience.

When we have faith, we can trust in the goodness of life and the universe, even in the face of adversity. It allows us to let go of our worries and fears and focus on the present moment, knowing that everything will work out for the best in the end.

Faith also helps us to cultivate a positive mindset, which is essential for overcoming fear. When we have faith, we can see the good in even the most difficult situations and find opportunities for growth and learning. This positive outlook not only helps us to overcome fear but also attracts more positive experiences into our lives.

However, having faith doesn't mean that we won't experience fear or that we should ignore our emotions. Fear is a natural response to uncertainty and danger, and it can be a helpful signal that something needs our attention. The key is to acknowledge our fears and then choose to have faith in ourselves and the world around us.

So how can we cultivate faith in our lives? Here are some practical tips:

1. Connect with a higher power: Whether you believe in God, the universe, or something else, connecting with a higher power can help you tap into a sense of faith and trust.
2. Practice gratitude: Gratitude is a powerful tool for cultivating faith and positivity. Take time each day to reflect on the things in your life that you are grateful for.
3. Surround yourself with positivity: Surrounding yourself with positive people, messages, and experiences can help you maintain a positive outlook and cultivate faith.
4. Take action: Taking action towards your goals and dreams can help you build confidence and faith in yourself.

5. Practice mindfulness: Mindfulness practices like meditation and yoga can help you stay present in the moment and cultivate a sense of inner peace and faith.

Having faith over fear is a powerful mindset shift that can help us overcome life's challenges with grace and resilience. By cultivating faith in ourselves and the world around us, we can learn to trust in the goodness of life and embrace all that it has to offer.

Fear and faith are two opposite emotions that have the power to shape our lives. Fear is a feeling that arises from a perceived threat, danger or uncertainty. It is an emotion that causes us to feel anxious, stressed and paralyzed. On the other hand, faith is a deep-seated belief in something that gives us the confidence and courage to overcome challenges and pursue our dreams. In this chapter, we will explore how faith can be the opposite of fear.

Faith is the Antidote to Fear

Fear is a powerful emotion that can have a profound impact on our lives. It can prevent us from taking risks, pursuing our dreams and living life to the fullest. However, faith is the antidote to fear. Faith gives us the courage to face our fears and overcome them. When we have faith, we trust that everything will work out in our favor. We believe that we are not alone and that there is a higher power that is guiding us towards our destiny.

Faith Helps Us to Let Go of Control

One of the reasons why fear is so powerful is that it is often rooted in our need to control the outcome of a situation. We fear the unknown because we cannot control it. However, when we have faith, we are able to let go of the need to control everything. We trust that everything will work out in the end, even if it is not in the way we expected. This helps us to approach challenges with a sense of calm and peace, rather than anxiety and stress.

Faith Provides Us with a Sense of Purpose

Another reason why faith can be the opposite of fear is that it provides us with a sense of purpose. When we have faith, we believe that there is a reason for everything that happens in our lives. We trust that there is a higher purpose to our existence and that we are part of something greater than ourselves. This belief gives us the motivation and inspiration to pursue our dreams, even in the face of adversity.

Faith gives us hope! When we have faith, we believe that there is always a light at the end of the tunnel. We trust that no matter how difficult our current situation may be, things will get better. This hope helps us to persevere in the face of challenges and to maintain a positive outlook on life.

Faith is the opposite of fear. While fear can paralyze us and prevent us from living our best lives, faith gives us the courage, confidence and motivation to pursue our dreams. By trusting in something greater than ourselves, we are able to let go of control, find our purpose, and maintain hope in even the darkest of times. The Bible is a timeless source of wisdom and guidance that has helped people for centuries to overcome their fears and find peace in the midst of difficult situations. Whether you are facing the fear of the unknown, the fear of failure, or the fear of death, the Bible offers valuable insights and practical advice that can help you face and conquer your fears. In this chapter, we will explore some of the ways that the Bible can help us to face and conquer our fears.

1. Seek God's presence and guidance

One of the most important things we can do when facing our fears is to seek God's presence and guidance. The Bible tells us that God is always with us and that we can trust Him to guide us through difficult times. Psalm 23:4 says, "Even though I walk through the darkest valley, I will fear no evil, for you are with me; your rod and your staff, they comfort me." When we seek God's presence and guidance, we can be confident that He will lead us through our fears and into a place of peace and security.

2. Find strength in God's promises

The Bible is full of promises that can give us strength and hope in the face of our fears. One of these promises is found in Isaiah 41:10, which says, "So do not fear, for I am with you; do not be dismayed, for I am your God. I will strengthen you and help you; I will uphold you with my righteous right hand." When we focus on God's promises and trust in His faithfulness, we can find the strength we need to overcome our fears.

3. Practice gratitude and praise

Another way the Bible can help us face and conquer our fears is by reminding us to practice gratitude and praise. When we focus on the good things that God has done for us, we can shift our perspective from our fears to God's goodness and faithfulness. Psalm 34:1 says, "I will extol the Lord at all times; his praise will always be on my lips." By praising God and giving thanks for His blessings, we can cultivate a spirit of gratitude and joy that can help us overcome our fears.

4. Learn from biblical examples

The Bible is filled with examples of people who faced their fears and overcame them with God's help. One of these examples is found in the story of David and Goliath in 1 Samuel 17. David was a young shepherd who faced the giant warrior Goliath with nothing but a sling and a stone. Despite his fear, David trusted in God's strength and defeated Goliath, becoming a hero to his people. By studying biblical examples like David, we can learn valuable lessons about facing our fears with faith and courage.

5. Seek support from a community of faith

Finally, the Bible reminds us of the importance of seeking support from a community of faith when facing our fears. Hebrews 10:24-25 says, "And let us consider how we may spur one another on toward love and good deeds, not giving up meeting together, as some are in the habit of doing, but encouraging one another—and all the more as you see the Day approaching." When we share our fears with others and seek their support and encouragement, we can find strength and courage to overcome our fears.

We can learn and strengthen ourselves from reading the Bible. The Bible offers a wealth of guidance and wisdom for facing and conquering our fears. By seeking God's presence and guidance, finding strength in His promises, practicing gratitude and praise, learning from biblical examples, and seeking support from a community of faith, we can overcome our fears and find peace in the midst of difficult situations.

18

OVERCOMING FEAR WITH GOD'S WORD

One of the most effective ways to overcome fear is through God's Word. The Bible is full of verses that encourage us to trust in God and not be afraid. Psalm 34:4 says, "I sought the Lord, and He heard me, and delivered me from all my fears." When we meditate on God's Word and speak it over our lives, we are strengthened and empowered to overcome fear. Overcoming fear with God's word. A Guide to Finding Courage, Strength, and Peace in the Midst of Fear.

Fear is a natural emotion that everyone experiences at some point in their lives. While it can be a helpful response to danger, it can also be a debilitating force that holds us back from living our lives to the fullest. However, as believers, we have access to a powerful tool that can help us overcome fear which is the will of God. Let's explore the nature of fear and its impact on our lives and discuss the different types of fear, from rational to irrational, and how they can affect us mentally, emotionally, and physically.

The power of God's Word to transform our lives. We will explore the Bible's teachings on fear, anxiety, and worry, and how they can help us overcome our fears. We will also discuss the role of prayer and faith in overcoming fear.The Bible contains many teachings on fear, anxiety, and worry. These teachings can help us overcome our fears by providing us with wisdom, guidance, and comfort. In this chapter, we will explore some of the key teachings on these topics and how they can help us to overcome our fears.

One of the most prominent teachings in the Bible on fear is the command to "fear not." This command appears throughout the Bible, and it is often accompanied by an assurance of God's presence and protection. For example, in Isaiah 41:10, we read: "Fear not, for I am with you; be not dismayed, for I am your God; I will strengthen you, I will help you, I will uphold you with my righteous right hand." Similarly, in Psalm 23:4, we read: "Even though I walk through the valley of the shadow of death, I will fear no evil, for you are with me; your rod and your staff, they comfort me."

These teachings remind us that God is always with us, even in the midst of our fears. We can take comfort in the fact that we are not alone, and that God is there to guide us and protect us. This can help to ease our fears and anxieties, and give us the strength we need to face our challenges.

Another important teaching in the Bible on fear is the importance of trusting in God. Proverbs 3:5-6 tells us, "Trust in the Lord with all your heart, and do not lean on your own understanding. In all your ways acknowledge him, and he will make straight paths." This teaching reminds us that we can trust in God's wisdom and guidance, even when we don't understand what is happening around us.

Trusting in God can also help us to overcome our fears by giving us a sense of perspective. When we trust in God, we are reminded that there is a bigger picture at work, and that our current struggles are only temporary. This can help to give us the strength we need to face our fears and move forward with confidence.

Finally, the Bible teaches us the importance of prayer and meditation in overcoming our fears. Philippians 4:6-7 says, "Do not be anxious about anything, but in everything by prayer and supplication with thanksgiving let your requests be made known to God. And the peace of God, which surpasses all understanding, will guard your hearts and your minds in Christ Jesus."

This teaching reminds us that we can turn to God in prayer and meditation when we are feeling anxious or afraid. By doing so, we can find a sense of peace and calm that helps to ease our fears and anxieties. Prayer and meditation can also help us to focus on God's presence and guidance, rather than on our fears and worries.

The Bible contains many teachings on fear, anxiety, and worry. These teachings can help us to overcome our fears by providing us with wisdom, guidance, and comfort. By trusting in God's presence and guidance, and by turning to him in prayer and meditation, we can find the strength and courage we need to face our fears and overcome them.

The Bible can help us find courage in the face of fear. We will explore the stories of David, Esther, and other biblical heroes who faced fear and overcame it with God's help. We will also discuss the importance of trusting in God's promises and relying on His strengthTrusting in God's promises and relying on His strength are essential elements of a meaningful and fulfilling life. The Bible is full of promises from God that offer hope and encouragement to those who believe. However, it can be challenging to trust in these promises, especially when we face difficult situations in life.

One of the most significant promises of God is that He will never leave us or forsake us. This promise is found in Hebrews 13:5, where it says, "Never will I leave you; never will I forsake you." This promise assures us that no matter what we face in life, we can trust that God is always with us, and He will never abandon us.

Trusting in God's promises requires faith. Faith is the assurance of things hoped for, the conviction of things not seen (Hebrews 11:1). We may not always see evidence of God's promises in our lives, but we must have faith that He is faithful and will fulfill His promises in His time.

Relying on God's strength is also crucial. We cannot rely on our own strength to navigate through life's challenges. We are human and limited, but God is all-powerful and can provide the strength we need. In Philippians 4:13, it says, "I can do all things through Him who gives me strength." This verse reminds us that we can accomplish anything with God's help.

When we rely on God's strength, we can face any obstacle with confidence. We don't have to be afraid because we know that God is on our side. He will provide the strength we need to overcome any challenge we face.

Trusting in God's promises and relying on His strength go hand in hand. We cannot have one without the other. When we trust in God's promises, we can rely on His strength to help us fulfill those promises. When we rely on God's strength, we can trust that He will provide what we need to overcome any obstacle and fulfill His promises in our lives.

Trusting in God's promises and relying on His strength are essential elements of a fulfilling life. We must have faith in God's promises, even when we don't see evidence of them in our lives. We must also rely on God's strength to help us overcome any obstacle we face. When we trust in God and rely on His strength, we can have the confidence to face any challenge and live a fulfilling life.

Finding Strength in God's Word will help you focus on how the Bible can help you find strength in times of fear. We will explore the teachings of Paul, who found strength in God's grace, and other biblical figures who drew strength from their faith. We will also discuss the importance of community and how it can provide us with the support we need to overcome our fearsThroughout the Bible, there are many examples of individuals who drew strength from their faith in God. One such figure is the Apostle Paul, who, through his teachings, showed how the grace of God can provide us with the strength to endure life's challenges.

Paul was a former persecutor of Christians who underwent a transformative experience on the road to Damascus, which led him to become one of the most influential figures in Christianity. In his writings, Paul emphasizes the importance of grace, which he defines as God's unmerited favor toward us.

In Paul's letter to the Romans, he writes, "For all have sinned and fall short of the glory of God, and all are justified freely by his grace through the redemption that came by Christ Jesus" (Romans 3:23-24). This passage emphasizes the idea that no one is perfect, but through God's grace, we can be saved.

Paul also writes about the importance of perseverance in the face of trials and tribulations. In his second letter to the Corinthians, he writes, "We are hard pressed on every side, but not crushed; perplexed, but not in despair; persecuted, but not abandoned; struck down, but not destroyed" (2 Corinthians 4:8-9). This passage illustrates how Paul draws strength from his faith in God, even in the midst of difficulties.

Another biblical figure who drew strength from his faith is Job. Job was a wealthy man who lost everything, including his family, possessions, and health. Despite his suffering, he remained faithful to God, declaring, "Naked I came from my mother's womb, and naked I will depart. The Lord gave and the Lord has taken away; may the name of the Lord be praised" (Job 1:21). Through his unwavering faith, Job was able to find strength in the midst of his suffering.

David, the shepherd boy who became the king of Israel, is another example of someone who found strength in God. In Psalm 23, David writes, "Even though I walk through the darkest valley, I will fear no evil, for you are with me; your rod and your staff, they comfort me" (Psalm 23:4). This passage illustrates how David relied on God's strength and protection, even in the midst of danger.

Teachings of Paul, along with the examples of Job and David, show us how we can find strength in God's grace. Through our faith, we can persevere in the face of trials and tribulations, and rely on God's strength and protection to guide us through life's challenges.

Finding Peace in God's Word can help you find peace in the midst of fear. Let's discuss the teachings of Jesus on anxiety and worry, and how we can apply them to our lives. We will also explore the importance of gratitude and mindfulness in overcoming fear and finding peace.

In times of fear, it can be difficult to find peace. The uncertainty of the future and the feeling of being out of control can overwhelm us. However, the Bible offers guidance and wisdom that can help us find peace in the midst of fear.

One of the most common messages in the Bible is the

commandment to not be afraid. This commandment is mentioned over 365 times in the Bible, one for each day of the year. This is because fear is a common human experience, but we are not meant to let it control us.

One of the most famous passages in the Bible that speaks to finding peace in the midst of fear is Psalm 23. This Psalm speaks of God as our shepherd who guides and protects us, even in the darkest valleys. The Psalmist writes, "Even though I walk through the darkest valley, I will fear no evil, for you are with me; your rod and your staff, they comfort me." (Psalm 23:4). This passage reminds us that even in the most difficult of times, God is with us, and we can find comfort and peace in His presence.

Another passage that speaks to finding peace in the midst of fear is Philippians 4:6-7. This passage encourages us to bring our anxieties to God in prayer, and promises that "the peace of God, which transcends all understanding, will guard your hearts and your minds in Christ Jesus." (Philippians 4:7). This passage reminds us that when we bring our worries and fears to God in prayer, He can give us a peace that goes beyond what we can understand.

Jesus also speaks about fear and anxiety. In Matthew 6:25-34, Jesus tells His followers not to worry about their lives, but to trust that God will provide for them. He says, "Therefore do not worry about tomorrow, for tomorrow will worry about itself. Each day has enough trouble of its own." (Matthew 6:34). This passage reminds us to focus on the present moment and trust that God will provide for our needs.

The Bible teaches us that we can find peace in the midst of fear by focusing on God's love. Romans 8:38-39 tells us that nothing can separate us from God's love, and that this love gives us the ultimate security and peace. It says, "For I am convinced that neither death nor life, neither angels nor demons, neither the present nor the future, nor any powers, neither height nor depth, nor anything else in all creation, will be able to separate us from the love of God that is in Christ Jesus our Lord." (Romans 8:38-39).

When you need peace in the midst of fear, read your bible for strength. It is your secret weapon. We are reminded to trust in God's presence and protection, to bring our worries and fears to Him in prayer, to focus on the present moment, and remember that nothing can separate us from God's love. By following these teachings and trusting in God, we can find peace even in the most difficult of times.

Fear is a natural and necessary emotion that helps us survive in dangerous situations. However, when fear becomes a constant presence in our lives, it can be debilitating and prevent us from living to our fullest potential. In order to overcome fear and find peace, it is essential to cultivate gratitude and mindfulness. Gratitude helps us focus on the positive aspects of our lives, while mindfulness allows us to be present in the moment and let go of anxious thoughts and feelings. In this chapter, we will explore the importance of gratitude and mindfulness in overcoming fear and finding peace.

- The Importance of Gratitude

Gratitude is the practice of focusing on the good things in our lives and being thankful for them. When we cultivate gratitude, we shift our focus from what we lack to what we have. This shift in perspective can have a profound impact on our mental and emotional wellbeing. Research has shown that people who practice gratitude experience less stress, anxiety, and depression than those who don't. Gratitude also improves our relationships, increases our happiness, and boosts our overall sense of wellbeing.

In the context of fear, gratitude helps us focus on the positive aspects of our lives, even when things seem scary or uncertain. When we are grateful for what we have, we are less likely to feel overwhelmed by fear and more likely to feel hopeful and optimistic about the future. Gratitude also helps us develop resilience, which is essential for overcoming fear. When we focus on the good things in our lives, we are better equipped to handle the challenges that come our way.

- The Importance of Mindfulness

Mindfulness is the practice of being present in the moment and paying attention to our thoughts, feelings, and sensations without judgment. When we are mindful, we are less likely to get caught up in anxious thoughts and feelings. We are also more able to let go of negative thoughts and emotions that contribute to fear and anxiety.

In the context of fear, mindfulness helps us become more aware of our thoughts and feelings and how they contribute to our fear. When we are mindful, we are better able to observe our thoughts and feelings without getting caught up in them. We can then choose to respond to our fear in a more productive way, rather than reacting to it impulsively.

- Gratitude and Mindfulness in Action

Here is an example of how gratitude and mindfulness can work together to help overcome fear:

Imagine that you are feeling anxious about an upcoming job interview. You start to worry about all the things that could go wrong and how you might fail. Your fear starts to feel overwhelming, and you can feel your heart racing and your palms sweating.

In this moment, you can practice gratitude by focusing on the positive aspects of your life. You might think about all the things you have accomplished in the past, the people who love and support you, or the things that make you happy. By focusing on the good things in your life, you can shift your perspective and feel more hopeful and optimistic about the future.

You can also practice mindfulness by becoming more aware of your thoughts and feelings. You might observe your anxious thoughts and feelings without judgment and let them pass without getting caught up in them. You can then choose to respond to your fear in a more productive way, such as by practicing deep breathing exercises or visualizing a successful interview.

Gratitude and mindfulness are powerful tools for overcoming fear and finding peace. By cultivating gratitude, we focus on the positive aspects of our lives and develop resilience, which is essential for overcoming fear. By practicing mindfulness, we become more aware of our thoughts and feelings and can choose to respond to our fear in a more productive way. When we combine gratitude and mindfulness, we create a powerful tool for managing fear and finding peace in even the most challenging situations.

The Bible can help us overcome specific fears, such as the fear of failure, the fear of rejection, and the fear of death. We will explore the stories of biblical figures who faced similar fears and overcame them with God's help. We will also discuss practical strategies for overcoming these fears.The Bible is a powerful resource that can help us overcome various fears, including the fear of failure, the fear of rejection, and the fear of death. In this chapter, we will explore how the Bible can help us face and conquer these fears.

- The Fear of Failure

The fear of failure is a common fear that can hold us back from pursuing our dreams and goals. It can cause us to feel inadequate, unmotivated, and discouraged. However, the Bible provides us with wisdom and encouragement to help us overcome this fear.

One of the most inspiring verses in the Bible is Philippians 4:13, which says, "I can do all things through Christ who strengthens me." This verse reminds us that we are not alone in our struggles, and we have the strength and power of Christ to help us overcome any obstacle or challenge.

Another helpful verse is Joshua 1:9, which says, "Have I not commanded you? Be strong and courageous. Do not be afraid; do not be discouraged, for the Lord your God will be with you wherever you go." This verse reminds us that we have God's support and guidance, and we should not be afraid to take risks and pursue our goals.

- The Fear of Rejection

The fear of rejection is another common fear that can hold us back from forming meaningful relationships and pursuing our dreams. It can cause us to feel unworthy, unlovable, and isolated. However, the Bible provides us with hope and reassurance that we are deeply loved and accepted by God.

One of the most comforting passages in the Bible is Romans 8:38-39, which reminds us that God's love for us is unconditional and unchanging, and we can never be separated from it.

Another helpful verse is Psalm 27:10, which says, "Though my father and mother forsake me, the Lord will receive me." This verse reminds us that even if we experience rejection from others, God will always be there to comfort and support us.

- The Fear of Death

The fear of death is perhaps the most universal fear, as it is a natural part of the human experience. However, the Bible provides us with hope and reassurance that death is not the end, but a gateway to eternal life with God. One of the most famous verses in the Bible is John 3:16, which says, "For God so loved the world that he gave his one and only Son, that whoever believes in him shall not perish but have eternal life." This verse reminds us that through faith in Jesus Christ, we can have the hope and promise of eternal life.

Another helpful verse is 1 Corinthians 15:55-57, which says, "Where, O death, is your victory? Where, O death, is your sting? The sting of death is sin, and the power of sin is the law. But thanks be to God! He gives us victory through our Lord Jesus Christ." This verse reminds us that even though death may seem like a defeat, through Christ, we have the ultimate victory over death. God gives us the wisdom, comfort, and hope to overcome our fears, including the fear of failure, the fear of rejection, and the fear of death. By relying on God's strength and guidance, we can face our fears with confidence and courage.

. . .

In the Bible, there are many stories of people who faced fears and overcame them with the help of God. These stories offer us inspiration and encouragement when we face our own fears and doubts. Here are just a few examples:

1. Moses: When God called Moses to lead the Israelites out of Egypt, Moses was afraid and doubted his ability to do what God was asking of him. But with God's help, he was able to perform miracles and lead the Israelites to freedom.
2. David: As a young shepherd boy, David faced the giant Goliath, who was feared by all the Israelites. But David trusted in God and defeated Goliath with just a sling and a stone.
3. Esther: Esther was a Jewish queen who risked her life to save her people from a plot to destroy them. She was afraid to approach the king without being summoned, but with God's help, she found the courage to do so and was able to save her people.
4. Daniel: Daniel was thrown into a den of lions because he refused to worship the Babylonian king as a god. He was afraid, but he trusted in God and was miraculously saved from the lions.
5. Mary: Mary was a young girl who was visited by an angel and told she would give birth to the Son of God. She was afraid and unsure of what this meant, but she trusted in God and accepted this task with humility and faith.
6. Paul: Paul was a persecutor of Christians until he had a miraculous encounter with Jesus on the

> road to Damascus. He was afraid to preach the gospel, but with God's help, he became one of the greatest evangelists in history.

There is a story of a woman who had an issue of blood for twelve years. This condition made her unclean according to Jewish law, and she was ostracized from society. The woman must have had fears about her condition and its impact on her life. She would have been scared of the physical pain and discomfort that came with the condition. Additionally, she would have been afraid of the social stigma and shame associated with it. Her condition would have made her ineligible to participate in religious activities, which would have caused her great distress. Despite her fears, she had faith that touching the hem of Jesus' garment would heal her, and her faith was rewarded. This story serves as an inspiration to women who may be facing similar fears due to medical conditions, and it highlights the importance of faith and hope in times of distress. These stories remind us that fear is a natural human emotion, but with faith in God, we can overcome it and do great things. We can trust in God's promises and rely on His strength to face our fears and overcome them. As it says in 2 Timothy 1:7, "For God gave us a spirit not of fear but of power and love and self-control."

Living a fearless life can be a daunting task, especially when we are surrounded by so many uncertainties and challenges. Fear of failure is one of the most common fears that hold us back from achieving our goals and living the life we desire. However, it is possible to overcome this fear and live fearlessly. In this chapter, we will discuss some strategies and techniques that can help you avoid the fear of failure and live a fearless life.

- Identify your fears

The first step to overcoming the fear of failure is to identify your fears. It is essential to understand what triggers your fear and acknowledge it. Once you have identified your fears, you can work towards overcoming them. Take some time to reflect on what causes your fear of failure. Is it a lack of confidence, fear of being judged, or fear of making mistakes? Once you have identified the cause, you can take steps to address it.

- Reframe your mindset

The way we think about failure can either fuel our fear or help us overcome it. Instead of thinking of failure as a negative outcome, reframe your mindset to see it as an opportunity to learn and grow. Remember that failure is not the opposite of success but a part of the journey towards success. Embrace your mistakes and failures and use them as stepping stones towards your goals.

- Set realistic goals

Setting unrealistic goals can often lead to fear of failure. When we set goals that are too high, we set ourselves up for disappointment and fear of failure. Instead, set realistic goals that challenge you but are achievable. This will help you build your confidence and reduce your fear of failure.

- Take small steps

Taking small steps towards your goals can help you build your confidence and reduce your fear of failure. Break down your goals into smaller achievable steps and celebrate each milestone. This will help you stay motivated and focused on your journey towards success.

- Focus on the process

Instead of focusing solely on the outcome, focus on the process of achieving your goals. Enjoy the journey towards success and celebrate each small victory. This will help you stay motivated and reduce your fear of failure.

- Surround yourself with positivity

Surrounding yourself with positive and supportive people can help you overcome your fear of failure. Seek out people who encourage and inspire you, and avoid those who bring you down. This will help you build your confidence and stay motivated towards your goals.

Remember we talked about taking care of your physical and mental health. It is essential in overcoming your fear of failure. Make sure you get enough sleep, eat a healthy diet, and exercise regularly. Practicing mindfulness, meditation, or yoga can also help reduce stress and anxiety.

Overcoming the fear of failure requires a mindset shift and a willingness to embrace mistakes and failures. By identifying your fears, setting realistic goals, taking small steps, focusing on the process, surrounding yourself with positivity, and practicing self-care, you can overcome your fear of failure and live a fearless life. Remember that failure is not the opposite of success but a part of the journey towards success. Embrace your mistakes and failures and use them as stepping stones towards your goals.

- Practical Strategies for Overcoming Fears

Fears are a natural and normal part of being human. Everyone experiences fear at some point in their lives. However, if fear becomes overwhelming and starts to interfere with daily activities and quality of life, it's time to take action. In this chapter, we'll explore practical strategies for overcoming fears and moving forward towards a more fulfilling life.

1. Identify the Fear

The first step in overcoming fear is to identify what exactly it is that's causing the fear. Sometimes fear can be rooted in past experiences or trauma. Other times, fear can be irrational and unfounded. It's important to recognize the difference between a real and imagined fear.

Once you've identified the fear, it's important to examine it closely. Ask yourself questions like:

- What specifically am I afraid of?
- How likely is this fear to come true?
- How will this fear affect my life if I don't confront it?

Answering these questions can help you understand the fear better and take steps to overcome it.

2. Take Small Steps

Confronting a fear head-on can be overwhelming and intimidating. Instead, try taking small steps towards facing the fear. For example, if you have a fear of public speaking, start by talking to a small group of people or recording yourself speaking and watching it back. Gradually increase the size of the audience or the difficulty of the speech until you feel comfortable speaking in front of a large crowd.

Taking small steps can help build confidence and gradually reduce the fear.

3. Use Visualization Techniques

Visualization techniques can be a powerful tool in overcoming fear. Visualization involves picturing yourself successfully facing and overcoming the fear. For example, if you have a fear of flying, imagine yourself boarding the plane, feeling calm and relaxed throughout the flight, and safely landing at your destination.

Visualization can help train the brain to respond differently to the fear and can help build confidence in facing the fear.

4. Seek Professional Help

If fear is impacting your daily life and preventing you from doing the things you want to do, it may be time to seek professional help. A therapist or counselor can help you identify the root cause of the fear and develop a plan to overcome it.

Therapy can also provide a safe space to discuss and process any past experiences or trauma that may be contributing to the fear.

5. Practice Self-Care

Fear can be stressful and exhausting. Practicing self-care can help reduce stress and anxiety and make it easier to confront the fear. Self-care can include activities like exercise, meditation, getting enough sleep, and spending time with loved ones.

Taking care of yourself can help build resilience and provide the energy needed to face and overcome the fear.

Overcoming fear takes time, patience, and effort. It's important to remember that everyone experiences fear at some point in their lives, and it's okay to ask for help. By identifying the fear, taking small steps, using visualization techniques, seeking professional help, and practicing self-care, it's possible to overcome even the most paralyzing fears and live a fulfilling life.

- Living Fearlessly

We have explored what it means to live fearlessly as believers. We discussed how we can cultivate a mindset of courage, strength, and peace, and how we can use God's Word to overcome any fear that may come our way. We will also explore the role of faith and trust in living a fearless life. Fear is a natural emotion that everyone experiences at some point in their life. Whether it's the fear of failure, the fear of the unknown, or the fear of something more specific, such as heights or spiders, it can be a paralyzing emotion that prevents us from reaching our full potential. However, by learning to live fearlessly, we can overcome our fears and achieve our goals.

Fear is an emotional response to a perceived threat or danger. It can be triggered by a wide range of stimuli, such as a loud noise, a dangerous situation, or a negative experience. Fear is a normal and natural response that serves to protect us from harm. It can help us to avoid dangerous situations and make better decisions. However, when fear becomes excessive or irrational, it can have a negative impact on our lives. It can prevent us from taking risks, pursuing our goals, and living our lives to the fullest. Fear can hold us back and keep us trapped in a cycle of anxiety and self-doubt.

Living fearless doesn't mean that we are never afraid. It means that we have learned to manage our fears and use them to our advantage. Living fearless means that we don't let our fears control us or hold us back. The first step in overcoming your fears is to identify them. What are you afraid of? Is it a specific situation, such as public speaking or flying? Or is it a more general fear, such as the fear of failure or rejection? Once you have identified your fears, it's important to understand why you feel that way. What is the underlying cause of your fear? Is it based on a negative experience or a belief that you have about yourself? The best way to overcome your fears is to face them. This doesn't mean that you should throw yourself into a dangerous situation, but it does mean that you should confront your fears in a safe and controlled way.

For example, if you have a fear of public speaking, start by speaking in front of a small group of people that you feel comfortable with. As you become more confident, gradually increase the size of your audience. Taking care of yourself is an important part of living fearlessly. When you are physically and emotionally healthy, you are better equipped to handle stress and manage your fears. Make sure that you are getting enough sleep, eating a healthy diet, and exercising regularly. Take time to do things that you enjoy, such as spending time with friends or pursuing a hobby.

Your mindset can have a big impact on how you perceive and react to your fears. Cultivating a positive mindset can help you to view your fears as challenges to be overcome rather than insurmountable obstacles. Always remember to practice gratitude and focus on the positive aspects of your life. Replace negative self-talk with positive affirmations. Surround yourself with positive people who support and encourage you.

Living fearless doesn't mean that you have to do it alone. Seek support from friends, family, or a professional counselor. Talking about your fears with someone who understands can help you to gain perspective and develop strategies for managing your fears. Also living fearless is about learning to manage your fears and using them to your advantage. By facing your fears, practicing self-care, cultivating a positive mindset, and seeking support, you can overcome your fears and achieve your goals. Remember, fear is a normal and natural emotion, but it doesn't have to control your life.

Practical Strategies for Overcoming Your Fears

Everyone experiences fear at some point in their lives. Whether it's fear of failure, fear of rejection, fear of the unknown, or fear of change, these emotions can be overwhelming and can hold us back from achieving our goals and living a fulfilling life. Fortunately, there are practical strategies that can help us overcome our fears and move forward with confidence.

Identify your fear and its root cause

1. The first step in overcoming your fear is to identify it and its root cause. Take some time to reflect on what specifically is causing you to feel fearful. Is it a past experience, a lack of knowledge or skills, or something else entirely? Understanding the underlying cause of your fear can help you develop a plan to overcome it.

Educate yourself

2. If your fear is related to a lack of knowledge or skills, then the best way to overcome it is to educate yourself. Take courses, read books, or find a mentor who can teach you what you need to know. The more knowledge and skills you have, the more confident you will feel in tackling your fear.

Break it down into smaller steps

3. Sometimes fear can be overwhelming because we try to tackle it all at once. To make it more manageable, break it down into smaller steps. Identify the first step you need to take, and focus on that. Once you have completed that step, move on to the next one. This will help you build momentum and confidence as you work towards overcoming your fear.

Practice mindfulness

4. Fear often arises from worrying about the future or dwelling on past experiences. Practicing mindfulness can help you stay focused on the present moment, which can reduce anxiety and fear. Take some time each day to practice mindfulness techniques such as meditation or deep breathing exercises.

Seek support

5. Overcoming fear can be challenging, and it's important to have a support system in place. Talk to friends or family members who can offer encouragement and support. Consider joining a support group or finding a therapist who can help you work through your fears.

Visualize success

6. Visualization is a powerful tool for overcoming fear. Take some time to visualize yourself succeeding in the face of your fear. Imagine how it will feel to overcome it and how it will impact your life positively. This can help you feel more confident and motivated to take action.

Take action

7. Ultimately, the best way to overcome your fears is to take action. Identify the steps you need to take and then take them. It's okay to feel scared or uncertain, but don't let those emotions hold you back. Remember, taking action is

the first step towards overcoming your fears and achieving your goals.

Overcoming fear is a process that requires patience, persistence, and a willingness to step out of your comfort zone. By identifying your fear, educating yourself, breaking it down into smaller steps, practicing mindfulness, seeking support, visualizing success, and taking action, you can overcome your fears and achieve your goals. Remember, you are capable of achieving great things, and fear should never hold you back from living the life you want.

In this chapter we have explored how the Bible can help us overcome fear and find courage, strength, and peace in the midst of it. Whether we are facing a specific fear or struggling with anxiety and worry, God's Word offers us a powerful tool for transformation. By trusting in God's promises and relying on His strength, we can live a fearless life and fulfill our God-given purpose.

19

THE POWER OF PRAYER

Prayer is another powerful tool for overcoming fear. When we pray, we are connecting with God and seeking His guidance and protection. Philippians 4:6-7 says, "Be anxious for nothing, but in everything by prayer and supplication, with thanksgiving, let your requests be made known to God; and the peace of God, which surpasses all understanding, will guard your hearts and minds through Christ Jesus." When we pray, we can experience the peace of God that surpasses all understanding. Prayer is an age-old practice that has been around for centuries. It is a way of communicating with a higher power, whether it is God, the Universe, or any other entity that you believe in. Prayer is a powerful tool that has the potential to bring about positive change in your life and the lives of those around you. In this chapter, we will explore the power of prayer and how it can benefit you.

Prayer is a form of communication that allows individuals to express their thoughts and feelings to a higher power. It can be done in different ways, such as reciting words or phrases, meditating, or simply sitting in silence.

Prayer can be done individually or in groups, and it can be practiced in different religions or spiritual practices. Prayer is a universal and deeply personal expression of communication with a higher power or divine entity. It is a way to connect with the divine, to seek guidance, comfort, or forgiveness, and to express gratitude and praise. Prayer has been a part of human culture and religion since the beginning of time and takes many different forms across different religions and spiritual traditions.

At its core, prayer is an act of faith and devotion. It is a way to acknowledge the presence of a higher power or divine force in our lives and to seek a deeper connection with that power. For many people, prayer is an essential part of their spiritual practice, providing a sense of peace, comfort, and direction in life. There are many different ways to pray, ranging from silent meditation to reciting formal prayers from a religious text. Some people pray alone, while others pray in groups or with a spiritual leader. Prayer can take place at any time or place, whether in a religious institution, at home, or in nature.

The purpose of prayer can also vary widely, depending on the individual and their spiritual beliefs. Some people pray to ask for help or guidance in difficult situations, while others pray to express gratitude for blessings and good fortune. Prayer can also be a way to seek forgiveness for past wrongs or to offer comfort and support to others in need.

One of the most important aspects of prayer is intention. When we pray, we are communicating with a higher power, and our intention and attitude can have a significant impact on the outcome of our prayers. It is important to approach prayer with an open heart and a spirit of humility, recognizing that we are not in control of everything in our lives and that we need help and guidance from a higher power.

Prayer is also a way to cultivate a deeper relationship with the divine. By regularly praying and seeking guidance from a higher power, we can develop a sense of spiritual awareness and understanding that can help us navigate life's challenges and find a sense of purpose and meaning. This deeply personal and meaningful expression of faith and devotion changes lives. It is a way to connect with a higher power, seek guidance and support, and cultivate a sense of spiritual awareness and understanding. Whether practiced alone or in community, prayer has the power to transform lives and provide a sense of peace and purpose in an uncertain world.

The power of prayer lies in its ability to bring about positive change in our lives. When we pray, we are tapping into a higher power that can guide us and help us to overcome our struggles. Prayer can give us strength, courage, and peace of mind, and it can also help us to connect with others and create a sense of community. There have been many studies that have explored the power of prayer, and the results have been positive. Prayer has been shown to reduce stress, anxiety, and depression, and it can also improve physical health. Prayer can also improve our relationships with others, as it helps us to cultivate empathy and compassion.

The multiple forms of prayer, and each one can be beneficial in its own way. Some people prefer to recite traditional prayers, while others prefer to speak from the heart. Some people pray alone, while others prefer to pray in groups. There is no right or wrong way to pray, and it is up to each individual to find the form of prayer that works best for them.

- The Five Benefits of Prayer

Prayer has many benefits that can help us to lead happier, healthier lives. Some of these benefits include:

1. ***Reducing Stress and Anxiety*** - Prayer can help us to reduce stress and anxiety by giving us a sense of peace and calm.
2. ***Improving Physical Health*** - Prayer has been shown to improve physical health by lowering blood pressure and reducing the risk of heart disease.
3. ***Cultivating Empathy and Compassion*** - Prayer can help us to cultivate empathy and compassion, which can improve our relationships with others.
4. ***Enhancing Spiritual Growth*** - Prayer can help us to deepen our spiritual connection and understanding, which can enhance our overall sense of well-being.
5. ***Creating a Sense of Community*** - Prayer can bring people together and create a sense of community, which can improve our social support and reduce feelings of loneliness.

Prayer is a powerful tool that has the potential to bring about positive change in our lives. It can help us to reduce stress, anxiety, and depression, and it can also improve our physical health. Prayer can help us to cultivate empathy and compassion, enhance our spiritual growth, and create a sense of community. Whether you pray alone or with others, the power of prayer is undeniable. So take a few moments each day to connect with a higher power and experience the benefits of prayer for yourself.

20

TRUSTING IN GOD'S PLAN

As Christians, we know that God has a plan for our lives. Jeremiah 29:11 says, "For I know the plans I have for you, declares the Lord, plans to prosper you and not to harm you, plans to give you hope and a future." When we trust in God's plan, we do not need to fear. We can be confident that God is working all things together for our good. We do not believe in fear because we have faith in God's power and love. We overcome fear by meditating on God's Word, praying, and trusting in God's plan for our lives. When we live in faith and not fear, we can experience the peace and joy that comes from knowing GodTrusting in God's plan can be a challenging concept to grasp, especially when faced with difficult circumstances or unexpected events. It requires a deep level of faith and surrender to the belief that everything happens for a reason and that ultimately, God is in control.

The idea of trusting in God's plan can be found in many religious texts, including the Bible. In Proverbs 3:5-6, it states, "Trust in the Lord with all your heart and lean not on your own understanding; in all your ways submit to him, and he will make your paths straight." This passage emphasizes the importance of trusting in God's wisdom and submitting to his will, even when we may not understand the reasons behind our circumstances.

Trusting in God's plan also requires a willingness to let go of our own desires and expectations. We may have specific goals or dreams that we want to achieve, but sometimes these plans do not align with God's will for us. In these situations, it can be challenging to trust that God has something better in store for us. However, it is essential to remember that God's plans are always greater than our own and that he has a purpose for every situation.

One way to strengthen our trust in God's plan is through prayer and meditation. By taking time to connect with God, we can seek guidance and peace in the midst of difficult circumstances. Prayer also helps us to acknowledge our limitations and recognize that we need God's help to navigate through life's challenges.

Another important aspect of trusting in God's plan is to have faith in his goodness. God's plan may not always be easy or comfortable, but we can trust that he is working for our good. In Romans 8:28, it says, "And we know that in all things God works for the good of those who love him, who have been called according to his purpose." This verse reminds us that even in difficult situations, God is working to bring about something good in our lives.

Trusting in God's plan also means accepting that we may not have all the answers. We may not understand why certain things happen, but we can trust that God has a purpose for everything. In Isaiah 55:8-9, it says, "For my thoughts are not your thoughts, neither are your ways my ways," declares the Lord. "As the heavens are higher than the earth, so are my ways higher than your ways and my thoughts than your thoughts." This passage emphasizes that God's wisdom is beyond our own and that we may not always understand his plan.

Trusting in God's plan is a challenging but essential aspect of our faith. It requires a willingness to let go of our own desires and expectations, a deep level of faith, and a recognition that God's ways are higher than our own. Through prayer, meditation, and faith in God's goodness, we can strengthen our trust in his plan and find peace in the midst of difficult circumstances.

Life can be unpredictable, and oftentimes we find ourselves in situations that we never could have anticipated. Whether it's a sudden job loss, a difficult diagnosis, or the loss of a loved one, these challenges can shake our faith and leave us feeling lost and hopeless. However, there are ways that we can strengthen our trust in God's plan and find peace in the midst of difficult circumstances.

One of the first steps we can take is to cultivate a daily practice of gratitude. When we take the time to reflect on the blessings in our life, no matter how small they may seem, it can help to shift our focus away from our problems and onto the goodness that surrounds us. This can be as simple as keeping a gratitude journal, where we write down three things we are grateful for each day, or taking a few moments each morning to reflect on the things we appreciate about our lives.

Another way to strengthen our trust in God's plan is to seek out support from others. This can mean reaching out to friends and family members, joining a support group, or seeking out the guidance of a spiritual leader. Oftentimes, talking through our problems with others can help us to gain new perspectives and find peace in the knowledge that we are not alone.

Prayer and meditation can also be powerful tools for finding peace in the midst of difficult circumstances. Whether it's through traditional prayer, mindfulness meditation, or another form of spiritual practice, taking the time to connect with our higher power can help us to find a sense of calm and clarity, even in the midst of chaos.

It's important to remember that we are not in control of everything. While we may feel helpless in the face of challenging circumstances, we can find peace in the knowledge that there is a larger plan at work. Trusting in God's plan, even when it is difficult, can help us to let go of our need for control and find peace in the present moment.

There are many ways that we can strengthen our trust in God's plan and find peace in the midst of difficult circumstances. By cultivating a daily practice of gratitude, seeking out support from others, practicing prayer and meditation, and letting go of our need for control, we can find comfort in the knowledge that we are not alone and that there is a larger plan at work. While life may be unpredictable, with faith and perseverance, we can weather any storm and emerge stronger on the other side.

All Things Work for Good

Romans 8:28 is a well-known and often quoted verse from the Bible, which says, "And we know that in all things God works for the good of those who love him, who have been called according to his purpose." This verse is a great comfort to believers, but what does it really mean? In this chapter, we will explore the meaning and implications of this verse.

The first thing to note is that the verse does not say that all things are good. In fact, many things that happen in our lives are not good. We experience pain, suffering, and loss. We struggle with sin and temptation. We face opposition and persecution. These things are not good in themselves, but God can use them for good.

The verse also does not say that everything will work out the way we want it to. We may pray for a particular outcome, but God may have a different plan. His ways are higher than our ways, and his thoughts are higher than our thoughts (Isaiah 55:8-9). We need to trust that God knows what is best for us and that he is working all things for our good. So, what does it mean that God works all things for our good? One way to understand this is to see it in light of God's sovereignty. God is in control of all things, and nothing happens outside of his will. This means that even the difficult and painful things we experience are part of his plan for our lives. He can use them to shape us, teach us, and grow us into the people he wants us to be.

Another way to understand this verse is to see it in light of God's grace. God is a loving and merciful God who wants what is best for us. He sent his Son, Jesus Christ, to die for our sins and reconcile us to himself. Through faith in Jesus, we are forgiven and adopted into God's family. We have the assurance that God is for us, not against us, and that he will work all things for our good. But what about the condition in the verse that says God works for the good of those who love him? Does this mean that only believers will experience God's goodness? Not necessarily. God is a gracious God who shows kindness and compassion to all people, even those who do not believe in him. However, those who love God have a special relationship with him. They have a deep and abiding love for him, and they seek to follow his will. As a result, they are more likely to recognize God's goodness and to experience his blessings in their lives.

What does it mean to be called according to God's purpose? This refers to God's plan for our lives. He has a specific purpose for each of us, and he calls us to fulfill that purpose. This purpose may involve different roles and responsibilities, such as being a parent, a spouse, a friend, a worker, or a servant of God. Whatever our calling may be, we can trust that God will work all things for our good as we seek to fulfill it.

Romans 8:28 is a powerful and comforting verse that reminds us of God's goodness and sovereignty. It assures us that even in the midst of difficult and painful circumstances, we can trust that God is working for our good. We can also have confidence that our lives have a purpose and that God is calling us to fulfill that purpose. Let us hold fast to these truths and trust in God's unfailing love and faithfulness.

21

THE POWER OF DAILY AFFIRMATIONS

Daily affirmations are positive statements that you repeat to yourself on a regular basis. These statements can be about anything that you want to improve in your life, such as your health, relationships, finances, career, or personal growth. The idea behind daily affirmations is that by consistently affirming positive beliefs about yourself and your life, you can reprogram your subconscious mind and improve your self-esteem, confidence, and overall well-being.

This book has explored the effects of daily affirmations and how they can help you achieve your goals and live a more fulfilling life. To understand how daily affirmations work, we need to look at the science behind them. According to the self-affirmation theory, people have a basic need to maintain a positive self-image. When people encounter situations that threaten their self-image, such as failure or rejection, they may experience negative emotions and a loss of self-esteem.

However, when people engage in self-affirmation, they can boost their self-esteem and reduce the impact of negative events.Affirmations are positive statements that people use to encourage themselves, build self-confidence, and enhance their well-being. They are a powerful tool for self-improvement and have been used by people for many years. The use of affirmations is often associated with spirituality, but the science behind affirmations is much more than that.

Affirmations work by creating new neural pathways in the brain. The brain is incredibly adaptable and can change its structure and function based on our thoughts and behaviors. When we think positive thoughts and affirmations, we activate the brain's reward center, which releases feel-good neurotransmitters like dopamine and serotonin.

Research has shown that positive affirmations can change the brain's neural pathways, making it easier to think positively and reduce negative self-talk. One study found that participants who practiced self-affirmations had increased activity in the brain's self-related processing regions, indicating a higher level of self-worth and self-esteem.

Another study found that affirmations can also reduce stress and anxiety. The researchers found that participants who practiced affirmations had lower cortisol levels (the stress hormone) compared to those who did not practice affirmations. This suggests that affirmations can help regulate the body's stress response and promote a sense of calm.

Affirmations can also be used to promote behavior change. When we affirm ourselves positively, we are more likely to act in ways that align with our positive beliefs. For example, if we affirm ourselves as healthy and fit, we are more likely to engage in healthy behaviors like exercise and eating well.

Studies have shown that affirmations can be effective in promoting behavior change. One study found that participants who practiced affirmations had higher levels of physical activity compared to those who did not practice affirmations. The researchers suggest that affirmations can help to strengthen the belief in one's ability to engage in physical activity, which in turn promotes actual behavior change.

Self-esteem is a crucial component of mental health and well-being. When we have positive self-esteem, we are more likely to feel confident, capable, and resilient. Affirmations can be a powerful tool for promoting self-esteem and self-confidence.

Research has shown that affirmations can improve self-esteem and self-confidence. One study found that participants who practiced self-affirmations had higher levels of self-esteem compared to those who did not practice affirmations. The researchers suggest that affirmations can help to reinforce positive beliefs about oneself, which can lead to greater self-esteem and self-confidence.

Resilience is the ability to bounce back from adversity and overcome challenges. Resilience is an essential skill for navigating life's ups and downs. Affirmations can be a valuable tool for promoting resilience. Research has shown that affirmations can promote resilience by increasing positive emotions, such as hope and optimism. One study found that participants who practiced affirmations had higher levels of hope and optimism compared to those who did not practice affirmations. The researchers suggest that affirmations can help to reframe negative situations in a more positive light, which can promote resilience.

The science behind affirmations is compelling. Affirmations can change the brain's neural pathways, promote behavior change, increase self-esteem and self-confidence, and promote resilience. Incorporating affirmations into your daily routine can be a powerful tool for promoting mental health and well-being. By affirming yourself positively, you can transform your thoughts, beliefs, and behaviors, leading to a happier, healthier, and more fulfilling life.

Studies have shown that daily affirmations can lead to improvements in mood, self-esteem, and well-being. In one study, participants who repeated positive affirmations for two weeks reported higher levels of self-esteem and lower levels of stress compared to a control group. Other studies have shown that affirmations can help reduce symptoms of depression and anxiety, improve academic performance, and even boost physical health.

There are many different types of affirmations that you can use to improve different areas of your life. Some common types of affirmations include:

- Positive self-talk: This involves replacing negative thoughts with positive ones, such as "I am capable and confident" instead of "I can't do this".
- Gratitude affirmations: These involve focusing on the things you are grateful for in your life, such as "I am grateful for my health, my friends, and my job".
- Future-focused affirmations: These involve visualizing and affirming a positive future outcome, such as "I will succeed in my career and achieve financial stability".
- Affirmations for specific goals: These involve creating affirmations that are tailored to a specific goal, such as "I am a successful entrepreneur who is making a positive impact in the world"

To reap the benefits of daily affirmations, it's important to practice them consistently and intentionally. Here are some tips for incorporating affirmations into your daily routine:

- Choose affirmations that resonate with you: Make sure your affirmations feel genuine and relevant to your life. You are more likely to stick with affirmations that you believe in.
- Repeat your affirmations daily: Consistency is key when it comes to affirmations. Set aside time each day to repeat your affirmations, whether it's in the morning, at night, or throughout the day.
- Use different mediums: You can write your affirmations down, say them out loud, or even record yourself saying them. Experiment with different mediums to find what works best for you.
- Believe in the power of affirmations: Remember that affirmations are a powerful tool for changing your mindset and improving your life. Believe in yourself and the process, and trust that your affirmations will have a positive impact on your life.

While daily affirmations can be a helpful tool for improving your mindset and well-being, it's important to acknowledge their limitations. Affirmations alone cannot solve all of your problems or guarantee success. It's also important to take action towards your goals and address any underlying issues that may be holding you back. Who are you and why do you exist? Who am I? Whose am I? And who he wants me to be and then go into different aspects of that so the first thing who am I? I am a child of the most high God!

Then you need to understand that and act accordingly, OK well that means! That God is my father and he has many mansions. I move accordingly to that and I believe who he is. Once I understand who I am, I'm able to maneuver differently. Things that people do, and say, don't affect me the way that they used to because I know who I am, and there's nothing that you can do to deter me from that or change me from that.

I am a fruitful Vine, and I was building on design in a certain way. It is not for everybody to understand and understand that you go through different trials and tribulations to get you where he wants you to be. Maybe you can't see the full picture because it develops as you go through different things. He may take you through several things, several different ways. He wants for you to get a different response and for you to get a true understanding of who you are!

So when we look at ourselves and young girls as they begin to grow and understand. Through learning themselves they're looking for things that haven't been giving to them. They look for these things in people and things that they can identify. However, at the end of today everyone is searching for love.

God is love his love is a love is indescribable because it's from someone that you've never seen but someone that you honor love and respect and that is able to do everything; but I feel you: he is a comforter, he's a healer, he's a provider, he's a doctor, he's a lawyer, he's the beginning, he's the end, he's alpha he's and omega. God has many names, and we should begin to understand that and know that he is our father. And he will do anything but fail.

You maneuver differently, you act different, you walk different, because you now know who you are and that's the beginning of knowing that you can do anything you can do anything. You put your mind to it doesn't matter what it is. I don't care what your mother said! Your father said people will say many things. I don't care about those things; it is your desire, and if it is his will, it is so done. And when you begin to walk in that.

Moving in that, you begin to know and understand who you are you're a child of the most high God, and sometimes you have to begin to access it and manifest those things in your life by saying them, and repeating them and that's why I'm such a fan of mantras and affirmations, because they begin to strengthen you, carve, and shape you into that person that you are. This is difficult to see when you're not in a place to understand. Inside you begin to understand who you are, you also will begin to go through many different things in trials, and that is testing your faith. It is testing your identity. It is testing the very means of who you are and for me that journey was quite difficult.

I was tested in many ways I was tested through adultery I was tested through manipulation. I was tested through abuse. I was tested through divorce of my parents, I was tested through Growing up with green grass in Inglewood and then having to move to the east side and the low bottoms of Compton Avenue and South Central. And that's a big shift; that's a big change for someone that comes from a middle-class family. To now live in poverty in the projects. There is no understanding! Who am I? This was a big identity change at a young age. This also was a trial and a test to get me to here and to where I am now. Understanding who I am! I'm grateful that God gives us these test and he's a forgiving God because some of us aren't forgiving and that's what makes our life so difficult.

It is because we are not forgiving when we do learn the value of forgiveness. And what forgiveness really is. As we begin to release some things we gain our strength, and power back. It's really about you gaining that strength and power by letting go whatever it is that you need to let go. Now when we talk about knowing who you are, you gain your identity, and you understand your worth!

People treat you different! People treat you the way you allow them to treat you! I need you to understand that. People, treat you the way you allow people to treat you! What I mean by that is. People can mistreat you, they could talk about you, they can misuse you, they can even abuse you.

They can also treat you how you desire them to treat you respectfully and that's is all decided on you. This is for all relationships! Business relationships, family relationships, in all relationships you have to gain respect by respecting yourself and enforcing how people respect you. We know this by the way we allow people to speak and treat you. So for the little girl or boy that is struggling in a relationship. When someone don't treat you, the way they should treat you. You should know that, this is not a healthy relationship for you to be in. You know this because God is love.

You deserve love! If someone is miss using you, this is harming you mentally or physically. This is not love! Most people who never say they love you. Or only say they love you after they hurt you. Do not know what love is and should be considered a danger to your health. If someone say that they love you after they hurt you, that is not love. If someone never says, I love you but claim that they do, this is not love, if someone is with you and claimed that they love you, but does not show it in front of others, this is not love.

Understanding love will help you begin to love and understand how people should treat you. How you enforce the way people to treat you is how you will be loved. For example, not just any one can approach me because of my demeanor. You must start to set healthy boundaries for yourself and communicate them effectively. This is important because it sends a message to others that you value yourself and expect to be treated with respect. When you allow people to approach you in a way that is consistent with your boundaries, you create the foundation for a positive and healthy relationship. This can apply to any type of relationship, whether it's a romantic relationship, a friendship, or a professional one. By being clear about your boundaries, you can weed out those who are not a good fit for you and attract those who are. Ultimately, it's important to remember that you have the power to shape the types of relationships you have by the way you allow others to approach you.

Once you begin to do these things and follow these guidelines, you will attract different type of people in your life. You will start to distance yourself from those people and environments that do not align with your values and goals. You will begin to seek out individuals and surroundings that challenge you to grow, learn, and become the best version of yourself.

When you understand your worth, you understand that your time and energy are valuable resources that should be invested in people and environments that uplift and support you. It takes courage and self-awareness to make these changes, but the rewards are worth it. You will start to see positive changes in your life, and you will begin to attract the people and opportunities that align with your values and goals. Remember, you are what you surround yourself with, so choose wisely.

If the things and people around us are not aligned with our aspirations, it can be challenging to achieve our goals. In such cases, it's essential to identify the aspects that are not aligned with our heart's desires and start taking steps to remove them from our lives. This may involve distancing ourselves from people who lack qualities such as empathy, humility, trustworthiness, and compassion, as they can have a negative impact on our own character development. Instead, we should aim to surround ourselves with individuals who exhibit the qualities we desire for ourselves and our children. By doing so, we create a positive environment that fosters growth and development and helps us achieve our desired outcomes. It's crucial to prioritize our well-being and surround ourselves with people who align with our values and vision for the future.

It is important to surround ourselves with positive and supportive people who lift us up and encourage us to be our best selves. However, there are also those individuals who exhibit negative and harmful behavior towards others, such as mistreating them or engaging in abusive behavior. These types of people are not conducive to a healthy and positive environment, and it is crucial to distance ourselves from them as soon as possible.

It is particularly concerning if these individuals exhibit abusive behavior towards their own family members, as it suggests a deep-seated lack of empathy and understanding of what love truly means. Therefore, it is important to always be vigilant and mindful of the people we surround ourselves with and make conscious decisions to remove ourselves from toxic situations and individuals who do not value or respect us or othersIt's important to understand that love is a complex and multifaceted emotion that can be expressed and experienced in many different ways. Unconditional love is often seen as the ideal, where love is given freely and without expectation of anything in return. However, in reality, it can be difficult to sustain this level of love in all circumstances.

In relationships, it's important to have a mutual understanding and reciprocation of love. If you're giving love to someone who isn't able to give it back, it may be time to reassess the relationship and consider moving on. It's not healthy to remain in a one-sided relationship where your needs are not being met.

That being said, it's also important to recognize that love is not always easy or straightforward. It may require compromise, forgiveness, and effort from both parties in order to maintain a strong and healthy relationship. Communication is key, and it's important to express your needs and expectations clearly to your partner.

Ultimately, it's up to each individual to determine what kind of love they want and deserve, and to take the necessary steps to cultivate and maintain that love in their lives.

The actuality of genuine, love is unconditional word it is not only giving it a show, and it should be replicated and if you're giving love, and someone else isn't replicating that and giving it back, remove yourself so you can Eventually have the love that you desire and still deserve but if you're with someone then it's not giving that doesn't even know what it is.

It's important to recognize the opportunities that come our way and to seize them with both hands. Sometimes, we may miss out on an opportunity because we're not paying attention or because we're too focused on other things. But if we keep our eyes and hearts open, we might just find that someone who can bring more abundance, love, and joy into our lives has just passed us by. And that's something we don't want to miss out on.

Furthermore, it's important to know who we are and what we deserve. As a child of the most high God, we have been promised all things. Our father has many houses and he is our shepherd, guiding us through life's ups and downs. When we identify who he is, we also identify who we are. We are children of the king of kings, and we deserve nothing but the best. By holding onto this belief and having faith, we can attract more abundance and love into our lives, and live our lives to the fullest.

He's Lord of Lord, he's ruler, he's alpha and omega. He's able to move and change any situation so there's nothing that I can go through, nothing that I can come across that he's not there with me he is in the midst, and he brings me peace. He brings joy. He brings love, he is not a confused man. He's not a fear he's not of hurt he's not in any of those things he is the great I am he is alba father And when you begin to know and learn who he is, there's nothing anyone on this earth can do or say to deter you from that so someone can't tell you that I love you and then beat you.

Someone can't tell you I love you and they mistreat you so much I can't say it because you know that God is love and his love is not shown or given in that way his love doesn't hurt his love is not a fear. His love is compassion and genuine and sincere and his love, his strength and power and so you're able to walk away from any situation that you're in and remove yourself because he's just that powerful at the sound of his name demons mostly try it the next time you come across a situation.

I dare you try it before they collar before you see it or

once, you're in it just say cheeses, five letter word just Jesus know Jesus is his son, but he gave his son to forgive you for all of your stand and you was hung ahead and he died, but our missions of your sense and so I dare you to stand up on his word as a believer, knowing that you are his child you are a child of the great I am you are, and he is your father and you can call you can scream You can whisper Jesus in Jesus and demons. Mostly they must move. God is amazing.

I want to talk about accessing who and whose you are through faith and Ness moving and speaking to those things that be is not as though they were this is the manifestation stage this is talking to your situation. This is speaking to your right circumstance, and this is standing and believing that God can do anything but fail. This is your interpretation of your new life, your new walk. Being he is, God will never give you more than you can bear. God will never leave or forsake you in order to strengthen these things.

I like to use mantras and some called them affirmations, but these are the tools that you need to get you in the mind-frame and in the space that empowers you to be better, trusting your faith and your walk will be extremely hard because now that you've accepted him into your life, and now that you know that he's your Lord and he's your savior, and now that you called him out for your father, and you've turned everything over to him that mean you no longer pick up things after you say I'm a let the Lord do it you leave it and you stand there and you know that he is the great I am, and he will do nothing but fail you And so Satan is real, and he comes in mini sizes in different forms and he will begin to attack you like he's never attacked you before in these attacks it's the test that you were going to have to pass in order to get where you need to be where he wants you to be Will it be easy no but can you do it yes why because you know who you are supported why because you know who you are interesting I think you got it in three and finally that's walking in it and standing and believing that you are what you say you are Mantras and your affirmation should be used daily as a new walkers.

I would say minimum of 3 to 4 times a day and that's repeating it and believing it and standing in it 3 to 4 times a day every day from the time you get up until the time you go to sleep so that's the phrase to a soon as you get up and then before you go to sleep that's two, but then at your mid day or maybe when you have lunch or you, Frazee something repeat it stand in it, believe it receive it and then maybe when you have dinner, repeat it stand in it believe it and then you will begin to understand that you are able you have the power that work within you and you will begin to know and understand my favorite Bible verse Ephesians 3:20 "Now unto to him who is able to do exceedingly and abundantly above all, we can ask or think, according to the power that worketh in us." Once you begin to access your Faith, you will begin to know and understand that you can do anything you put your mind to do.

So know that saying and repeating daily affirmation is sewing good fruit into yourself and producing great things. The key is to just start! Let's start together simply by saying, I am beautiful, I am who God wants me to be, I have been designed uniquely and creatively in his image. I am strong and powerful and I'm getting better in every way! If you believe and receive the word of God, begin to heal yourself every day by simply repeating and saying this four times a day.

The Effects of Change in 21 Consecutive Days

Change is an inevitable aspect of life. It is an essential ingredient for personal growth, development, and success.

The idea of change often comes with a sense of discomfort and uncertainty, which can make it challenging to implement. However, research has shown that small changes made consistently over a period of time can lead to significant improvements in our lives.

The concept of 21 consecutive days has become a popular benchmark for making changes in our lives. It is believed that if we can commit to making a change consistently for 21 days, it will become a habit, and it will be easier to maintain. But what are the effects of change in 21 consecutive days?

Positive Effects of Change in 21 Consecutive Days !

1. Improved Mental Health: Making a change, no matter how small, can have a significant impact on our mental health. When we commit to making positive changes in our lives, it can lead to a sense of accomplishment and self-worth, which can help reduce stress and anxiety.
2. Increased Productivity: Implementing a change consistently for 21 consecutive days can improve our productivity levels. When we make changes to our daily routine, we become more efficient in our work, and this can lead to increased productivity.
3. Better Physical Health: Making changes to our lifestyle, such as exercising regularly or eating a balanced diet, can improve our physical health. When we commit to making these changes for 21 consecutive days, they become habits, and we are more likely to continue with them in the long run.

4. Improved Relationships: Making changes to our behavior or communication styles can have a positive impact on our relationships. When we commit to making changes consistently for 21 days, it can lead to better communication and understanding, which can strengthen our relationships.
5. Increased Self-Discipline: Committing to making a change for 21 consecutive days requires self-discipline. When we practice self-discipline consistently, it can spill over into other areas of our lives, leading to increased self-control and willpower.

Negative Effects of Change in 21 Consecutive Days

1. Burnout: Committing to making a change for 21 consecutive days can be challenging, especially if the change requires a significant amount of effort or time. This can lead to burnout, where we become exhausted and lose motivation to continue.
2. Resistance to Change: Some people may find it difficult to make changes to their lives, and committing to doing so for 21 consecutive days may feel overwhelming. This can lead to resistance to change, where people feel unmotivated or unwilling to make the necessary changes.
3. Frustration: When we commit to making a change for 21 consecutive days and do not see the results we were hoping for, it can be frustrating. This can lead to a sense of disappointment and

discouragement, which can make it difficult to continue with the change.

Committing to making a change for 21 consecutive days can have a significant impact on our lives. It can lead to improved mental and physical health, increased productivity, better relationships, and increased self-discipline. However, it is essential to be aware of the potential negative effects, such as burnout, resistance to change, and frustration. When making changes, it is important to set realistic goals and expectations and to celebrate small wins along the way. With consistency and persistence, even small changes can lead to significant improvements in our lives.

The Power of Mantras

Mantras are sacred sounds, words, or phrases that are chanted or repeated in a rhythmic and melodic manner. They have been used for centuries in spiritual practices, particularly in Hinduism and Buddhism, to achieve various goals such as enlightenment, healing, and inner peace.

The word "mantra" comes from the Sanskrit language and is derived from two words - "manas" meaning mind and "tra" meaning tool or instrument. Thus, a mantra is considered a tool or instrument of the mind that helps to focus the mind, calm the emotions, and connect with the divine.

There are many types of mantras, each with its own unique vibration and purpose. Some mantras are used for healing and physical wellbeing, while others are used for spiritual growth and enlightenment. Here are some examples of popular mantras and their meanings:

The power of mantras lies in their vibration and resonance. When we chant or repeat a mantra, we create a vibration in our body and mind that helps to align our energy with the divine. This alignment can bring about profound changes in our physical, emotional, and spiritual wellbeing.

Scientific studies have also shown the benefits of chanting mantras. Chanting mantras has been found to reduce stress and anxiety, lower blood pressure, improve concentration and focus, and promote a sense of wellbeing and happiness.

One of the key benefits of chanting mantras is that it helps to quiet the mind and reduce mental chatter. The repetitive nature of chanting a mantra helps to create a sense of focus and concentration, which can lead to a deeper state of meditation.

Another benefit of chanting mantras is that it helps to create a positive vibration and energy field around us. This positive energy can help to attract positive people and situations into our lives and repel negativity and stress.

Mantras are powerful tools for spiritual growth and wellbeing. By chanting or repeating a mantra, we can connect with the divine, quiet the mind, and promote inner peace and harmony. So, if you are looking for a way to improve your physical, emotional, and spiritual wellbeing, try incorporating mantras / affirmations.

Chapter: Repeating Positive Affirmation - I Am a Fruitful Vine

Positive affirmations are powerful tools that can help you to overcome negative self-talk and cultivate a positive mindset. By repeating affirmations that focus on your strengths, you can build confidence and self-esteem, and improve your overall well-being. One such affirmation that can help you to achieve this is "I am a fruitful vine."

This affirmation is based on the biblical reference in Psalms 128:3, which reads "Your wife will be like a fruitful vine within your house; your children will be like olive shoots around your table." This verse speaks of the blessings that come to those who live in accordance with God's will. It is a reminder that when we are rooted in faith and goodness, we will bear fruit and prosper in all areas of our lives.

When we repeat the affirmation "I am a fruitful vine," we are affirming our connection to the divine and acknowledging that we are capable of bearing fruit and living a prosperous life. This affirmation can be especially powerful when we are facing challenges or feeling stuck, as it reminds us that we have the potential to grow and thrive.

To begin using this affirmation, find a quiet and comfortable place where you can sit or lie down without distractions. Take a few deep breaths to center yourself and then repeat the affirmation to yourself, either silently or out loud. As you repeat the affirmation, visualize yourself as a strong and healthy vine, with branches reaching out and bearing fruit.

Try to focus on the feeling of abundance and prosperity that comes with being a fruitful vine. If your mind wanders, gently bring it back to the affirmation and the image of yourself as a thriving vine. You can repeat this affirmation as often as you like, but it's best to do it daily, ideally in the morning to set the tone for your day.

In addition to repeating the affirmation, you can also take practical steps to cultivate a fruitful life. This may include setting goals, developing healthy habits, and surrounding yourself with positive influences. By combining the power of positive affirmation with action, you can create a life that is full of abundance and joy.

"I am a fruitful vine" is a powerful positive affirmation that can help you to cultivate a positive mindset and achieve your goals. By repeating this affirmation daily and visualizing yourself as a thriving vine, you can tap into your potential for growth and prosperity. Remember that the key to success is not just in repeating the affirmation, but also in taking practical steps towards a fruitful life. With dedication and effort, you can transform your life and become a truly fruitful vine.

Joseph, the eleventh son of Jacob, is described in the book of Genesis as a fruitful vine. This metaphorical language is used to describe Joseph's character, his life journey, and his contributions to the growth and prosperity of his family and community.

The metaphor of a fruitful vine is a powerful image in the Bible. It is used to describe the people of Israel in many places, such as in Psalm 80:8: "You brought a vine out of Egypt; you drove out the nations and planted it." In the context of Joseph's story, the metaphor is used to highlight his unique role as a leader and provider for his family.

Joseph's journey begins with a dream in which he sees himself as a fruitful vine, with branches spreading out and bearing fruit. This dream is a premonition of Joseph's future success and the ways in which he will provide for his family and community. It is also a reminder of the important role that he will play in fulfilling the covenant that God made with his ancestors.

Joseph's journey is not an easy one. He is sold into slavery by his jealous brothers and taken to Egypt. However, even during hardship and adversity, Joseph remains steadfast in his faith and continues to grow and thrive. He rises to become the chief steward of his master's household, and later the second-in-command of all of Egypt.

Through his wisdom and foresight, Joseph can provide for his family during a time of famine, and to ensure their survival for generations to come. He is also able to use his position of power to help the people of Egypt and to promote justice and prosperity in the land.

Joseph's story is a powerful reminder of the importance of faith, perseverance, and generosity. Like a fruitful vine, he grows and spreads, providing nourishment and sustenance to those around him. His story is also a reminder of the ways in which God uses our struggles and challenges to shape us and to bring about his plans and purposes.

In the end, Joseph's story is one of redemption and reconciliation. He is reunited with his brothers, forgives them for their past mistreatment of him, and brings his family back together. Through his example, we are reminded of the power of forgiveness and the importance of working towards unity and peace in our own lives and communities.

Joseph's story is a testament to the power of a fruitful vine. Through his faith, perseverance, and generosity, he was able to grow and thrive, and to provide for his family and community. His story is a reminder of the importance of remaining steadfast in our faith and of the ways in which God uses us to bring about his plans and purposes.

22

MANTRA CHALLENGE

8 Step 21-day "Mantra" challenge to improve, encourage, and change your life:

Step 1: Choose a mantra that resonates with you and reflects the changes you want to see. It can be a positive affirmation or a statement that inspires you. Write it down on a piece of paper and keep it handy.

Step 2: Find a clean and empty jar with a lid. This jar will be your "mantra jar." Place it somewhere you can see it every day, like on your bedside table or your desk.

Step 3: Open your heart and connect with your inner self. Take a deep breath and visualize the changes you want to see. Allow yourself to feel the emotions associated with those changes.

Step 4: Say your chosen mantra out loud three times. Believe with your heart that you can complete the goal of reading and memorizing the mantra out loud every day for 21 days.

Step 5: Close the lid of the jar, sealing in your intentions and declaring victory over your doubts. You have committed to this challenge, and you will see it through.

Step 6: Every day for the next 21 days, open the jar, take out the paper with your mantra, and read it, out loud three times. Take a moment to reflect on the mantra's meaning and how it applies to your life.

Step 7: After you have completed your 21-day challenge, take a moment to reflect on the changes you have experienced. You may have noticed a shift in your thoughts, emotions, and actions. You may have achieved some of the goals you set for yourself. Acknowledge and celebrate your progress.

Step 8: Repeat the challenge if desired or choose a new mantra to focus on. The more you practice this challenge, the more you will see the power of God working in you to improve, encourage, and change your life.

"My past mistakes serve as the fuel to my burning desire to become better. With an open heart and open hands, I am ready to receive any type of blessing that comes my way."

You Can Do It ! Access Your Faith ! Let's Go !

Made in the USA
Columbia, SC
14 November 2023

c672f5c4-554a-4739-9045-3f79b0b9d33cR02